Disney LEARNING

From the movie
Disney
FROZEN

AGES
6-7
KEY STAGE 1

Adding and Subtracting

SCHOLASTIC

Scholastic Children's Books
Euston House,
24 Eversholt Street,
London NW1 1DB, UK

A division of Scholastic Ltd
London ~ New York ~ Toronto ~ Sydney ~ Auckland
Mexico City ~ New Delhi ~ Hong Kong

This book was first published in Australia in 2014 by Scholastic Australia.
Published in the UK by Scholastic Ltd, 2015

ISBN 978 1 4071 6286 7

Printed in United Kingdom by Bell and Bain Ltd, Glasgow

6 8 10 9 7

Parent Letter

Welcome to the Disney Learning Programme!

Children learn best when they are having fun! The **Disney Learning Workbooks** are an engaging way for your child to explore basic maths along with fun characters from the wonderful world of Disney.

The **Disney Learning Workbooks** are carefully levelled to present new challenges to developing learners. Designed to support the National Curriculum for Maths at Key Stage 1, they offer your child the opportunity to practise skills learned at school and to consolidate their learning in a relaxed home setting with support from you. With stickers, games, speed challenges and flash cards, your child will have fun learning basic maths!

Number confidence is key to the primary National Curriculum for Mathematics. The activities in this book will help your child learn basic maths facts and use them to solve more difficult additions and subtractions. Strategies such as counting on or back, rearranging number sentences and organising number facts into families will help your child become confident in recalling maths facts, allowing them to devote more mental energy to solving more complex maths problems quickly and confidently.

Throughout the book you will also find 'Let's Read' stories featuring the characters from the Disney movie *Frozen* for you to enjoy sharing with your child. Reading for pleasure and enjoying books together is a fundamental part of learning. Keep sessions fun and short. Your child may wish to work independently on some of the activities or you may enjoy doing them together – either way is fine.

Have fun with the Disney Learning programme!

Developed in conjunction with Catherine Baker, Educational Consultant

Let's Learn Maths Facts

This book is full of activities based on different maths fact strategies. The more strategies you practise, the more quickly and accurately you will add and subtract!

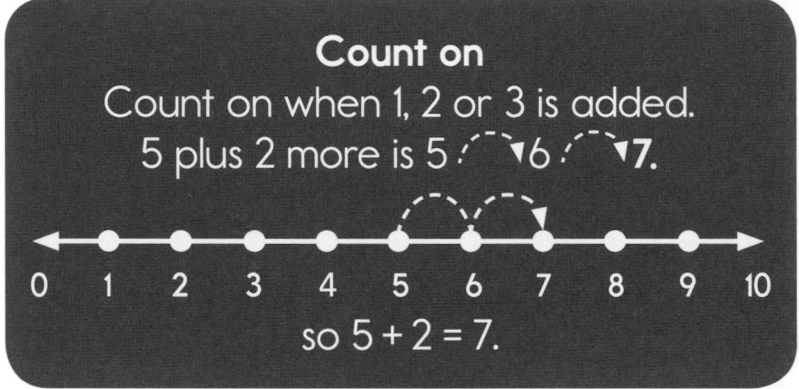

Count on
Count on when 1, 2 or 3 is added.
5 plus 2 more is 5 6 **7.**

0 1 2 3 4 5 6 7 8 9 10

so 5 + 2 = 7.

Count back
Count back when 1, 2 or 3 is subtracted.
5 take away 2 is 5 4 **3.**

0 1 2 3 4 5 6 7 8 9 10

so 5 – 2 = 3.

Rearrange number sentences

If you know that 4 + 6 = 10, then you know that 6 + 4 = 10.

Fact families

The same three numbers make two addition facts and two subtraction facts. This is a fact family.

2 + 3 = 5   5 – 3 = 2
3 + 2 = 5   5 – 2 = 3.

Doubles

Use doubles to find doubles plus 1.
So if you know
5 + 5 = 10, then you know that
5 + 6 = 11, 10 – 5 = 5 and 11 – 5 = 6.

Larger facts

Use the facts you know to answer harder questions. If you know
2 + 3 = 5, then you know that
20 + 30 = 50.

Not long ago, in the Kingdom of Arendelle, Princess Elsa and Princess Anna were playing. Elsa had magical powers and could create things out of ice! She made a snowman called Olaf.

While the girls were playing, Elsa accidentally hit Anna with an icy blast. Anna was hurt and lost her memory. She forgot all about Elsa's magic.

From then on, whenever Elsa had strong feelings, the magic spilled out. Elsa never wanted to hurt her sister again, so she stayed away from Anna.

Years later, it was time for Elsa to become queen. She was terrified. What if something happened and she lost control of her powers?

Anna was excited. She met a handsome prince called Hans.

After Elsa became queen, Anna told her that she wanted to marry Hans. Elsa forbade it. How could Anna want to marry a man she had only just met?

The two sisters argued and Elsa became so upset that ice and snow blasted from her hand across the ballroom. Her secret powers were exposed!

Afraid that she might hurt her people, Elsa fled.

Let's Make Numbers

Colour the circles blue and purple to show two different ways to make the number. The first one is done for you.

7	●●●●●●● __4__ and __3__
7	◯◯◯◯◯◯◯ __5__ and __2__
8	◯◯◯◯◯◯◯◯ __7__ and __1__
8	◯◯◯◯◯◯◯◯ __4__ and __4__
9	◯◯◯◯◯◯◯◯◯ __8__ and __1__
9	◯◯◯◯◯◯◯◯◯ __5__ and __4__

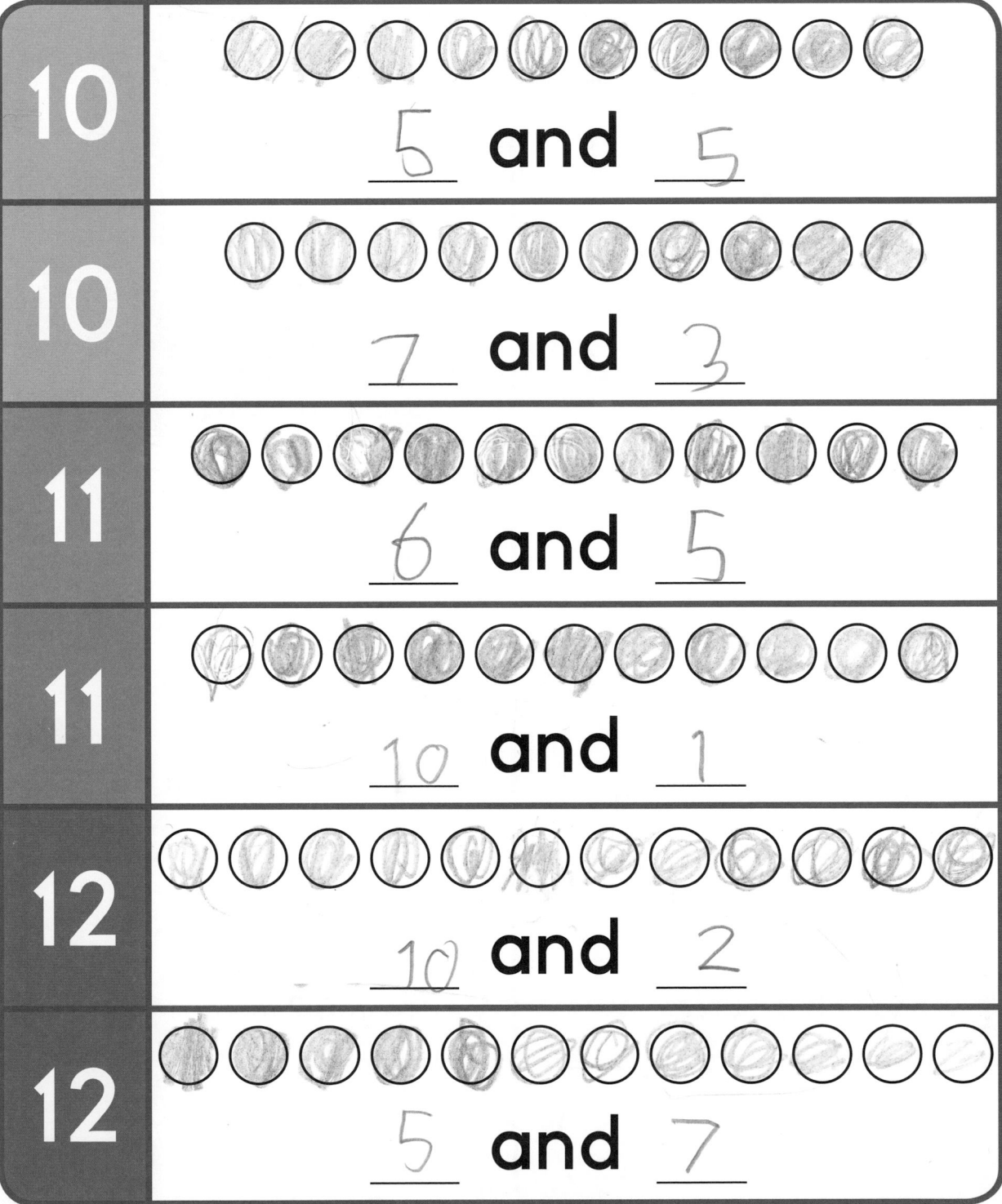

10	5 and 5
10	7 and 3
11	6 and 5
11	10 and 1
12	10 and 2
12	5 and 7

Let's Add

Read the problem.
Write the answer.
The first one is done for you.

There are 2  .

Elsa gets 2 more.

How many in total?

__2__ and __2__ more is __4__ .

There are 5  .

Elsa gets 1 more.

How many in total?

___ and ___ more is ___ .

There are 4 .

Olaf gets 2 more.

How many in total?

___ and ___ more is ___ .

There are 6  .

Anna gets 3 more.

How many in total?

___ and ___ more is ___ .

There are 7  .

Hans gets 2 more.

How many in total?

___ and ___ more is ___ .

There are 4 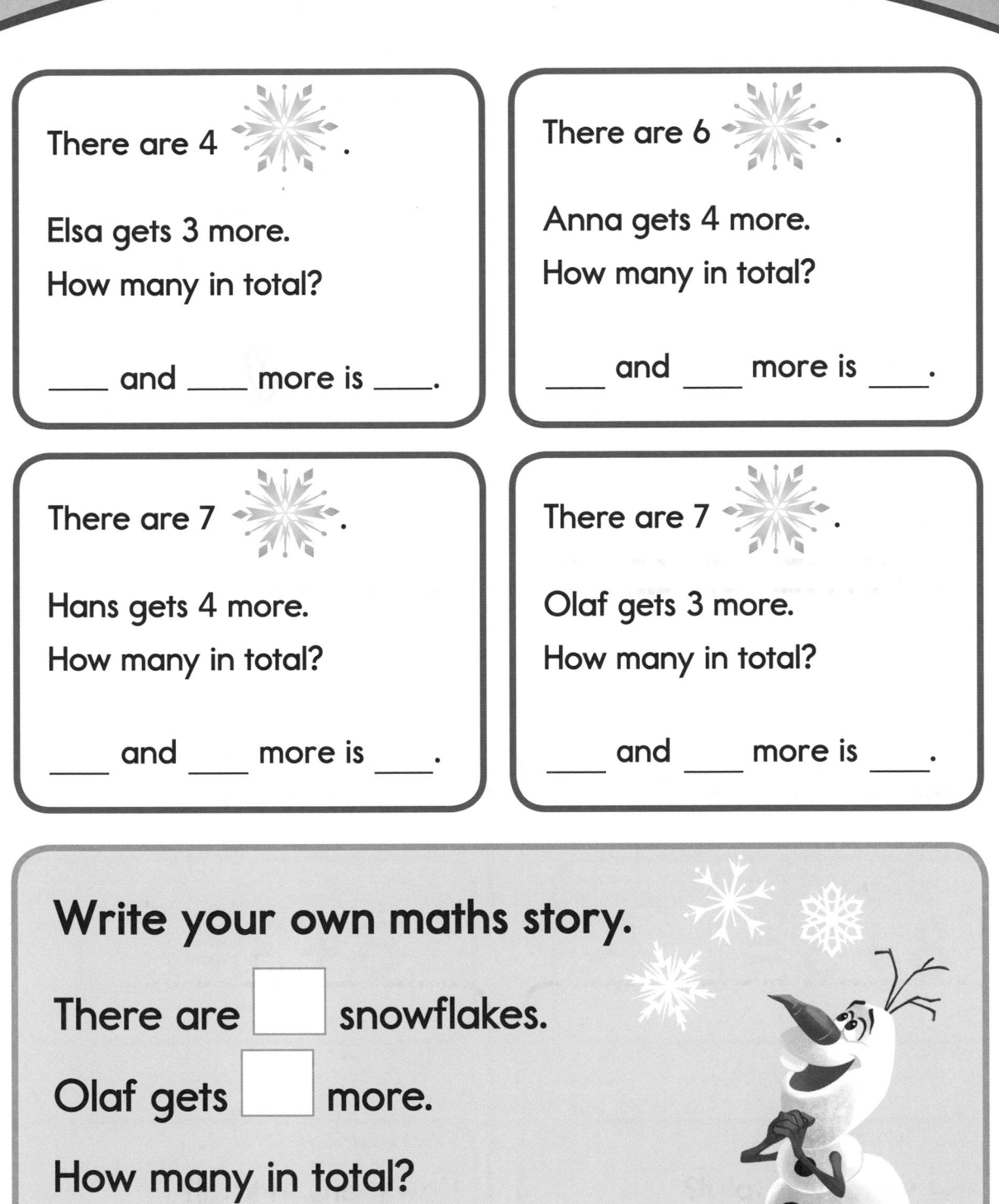 .

Elsa gets 3 more.

How many in total?

____ and ____ more is ____ .

There are 6 .

Anna gets 4 more.

How many in total?

____ and ____ more is ____ .

There are 7 .

Hans gets 4 more.

How many in total?

____ and ____ more is ____ .

There are 7 .

Olaf gets 3 more.

How many in total?

____ and ____ more is ____ .

Write your own maths story.

There are ☐ snowflakes.

Olaf gets ☐ more.

How many in total?

☐ and ☐ more is ☐ .

Let's Count On to Add

Count on to add. Use the number line to help.
Write the sum.
The first one is done for you.

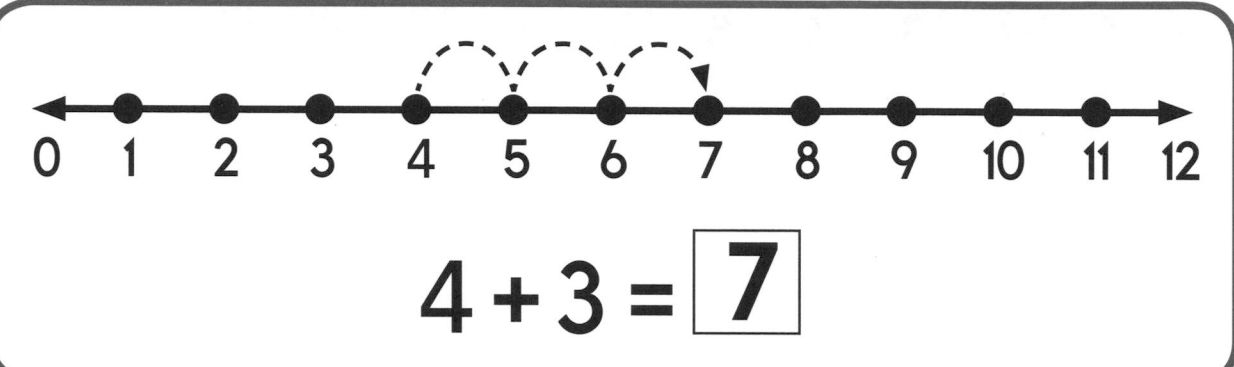

$$4 + 3 = \boxed{7}$$

$6 + 2 = \square$

$3 + 2 = \square$

$8 + 3 = \square$

$5 + 3 = \square$

$11 + 1 = \square$

$9 + 3 = \square$

Count on to add. Use
the number line to help.
Write the sum.

0 1 2 3 4 5 6 7 8 9 10 11 12

6 + 1 = ☐

7 + 2 = ☐

10 + 2 = ☐

3 + 3 = ☐

Let's Rearrange
Number Sentences

Count the numbers on the dice. Write the sum.
Now rearrange the number sentence. The first one is done for you.

6 + 3 = 9
3 + 6 = 9

2 + 4 = ☐
4 + 2 = ☐

4 + 6 = ☐
6 + 4 = ☐

3 + 2 = ☐
2 + 3 = ☐

4 + 1 = ☐
1 + 4 = ☐

Try this:

If you know 7 + 1 = 8,

then you know ☐ + ☐ = ☐

5 + 2 = ☐
2 + 5 = ☐

1 + 5 = ☐
5 + 1 = ☐

4 + 5 = ☐
5 + 4 = ☐

3 + 5 = ☐
5 + 3 = ☐

5 + 6 = ☐
6 + 5 = ☐

Try this:

If you know 3 + 4 = 7,

then you know ☐ + ☐ = ☐

Let's Add 5

Add the counters.
Write the sum.
The first one is done for you.

3 + 5 = __8__

1 + 5 = ___

2 + 5 = ___

4 + 5 = ___

0 + 5 = ___

Let's Colour

Colour the counters.
Write the sum.
The first one is done for you.

6 + 2 = __8__

7 + 1 = ___

6 + 3 = ___

8 + 1 = ___

7 + 2 = ___

Let's Add
Larger Numbers

Write the sum.
The first one is done for you.

$10 + 9 = \boxed{19}$

$17 + 2 = \square$

$15 + 1 = \square$

$18 + 2 = \square$

$12 + 4 = \square$

$10 + 5 = \square$

$13 + 5 = \square$

❄ Super-duper Sums: ❄

$100 + 9 = \boxed{}$

$150 + 1 = \boxed{}$

Let's Add
Three Numbers

Count on to add three numbers.
Use the number line to help.
Write the sum. The first one is done for you.

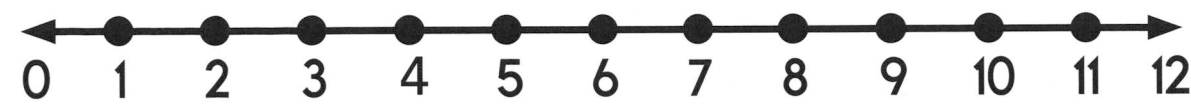

0 1 2 3 4 5 6 7 8 9 10 11 12

$5 + 3 + 1 =$ 9

$2 + 2 + 3 =$ ☐

$6 + 1 + 2 =$ ☐

$2 + 5 + 1 =$ ☐

$4 + 1 + 2 =$ ☐

$7 + 2 + 1 =$ ☐

$4 + 3 + 1 =$ ☐

$5 + 2 + 2 =$ ☐

❄ Super-duper Sums: ❄

$50 + 30 + 10 =$ ☐

$20 + 20 + 30 =$ ☐

Let's Race

Solve the problems to help Anna chase after Elsa.
Record your time and the number of correct answers.
On your marks, get set, go!

6 + 4 =	7 + 3 =	5 + 6 =	2 + 9 =
4 + 2 =	3 + 3 =	8 + 4 =	3 + 6 =
6 + 3 =	0 + 8 =	9 + 3 =	12 + 3 =
8 + 3 =	2 + 3 =	7 + 2 =	1 + 3 =
10 + 6 =	3 + 4 =	3 + 2 =	1 + 7 =
6 + 2 =	4 + 5 =	10 + 2 =	4+3+2=

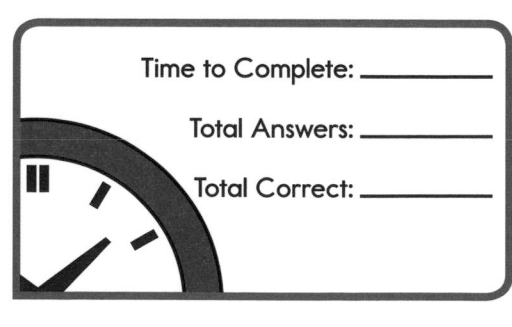

Time to Complete: _____

Total Answers: _____

Total Correct: _____

Keep it up!
See if you can beat your score.
On your mark, get set, go!

4 + 1 =	7 + 5 =	0 + 2 =	2 + 4 =
17 + 3 =	4 + 7 =	2 + 7 =	1 + 6 =
4 + 3 =	8 + 1 =	4 + 1 + 3 =	8 + 2 =
5 + 3 =	7 + 4 =	12 + 5 =	6 + 2 + 1 =
1 + 2 =	5 + 7 =	4 + 6 =	3 + 3 + 2 =
10 + 1 =	5 + 1 =	4 + 4 =	2 + 6 =

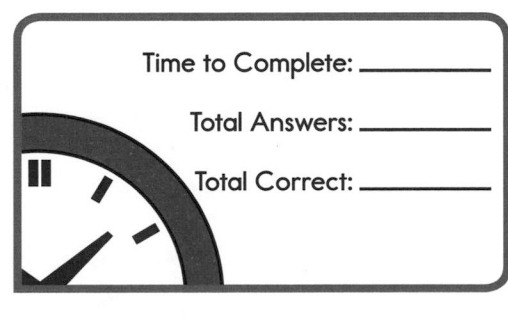

Time to Complete: _____

Total Answers: _____

Total Correct: _____

Let's Read

At last Anna understood why Elsa had kept to herself for so many years. She rushed off to the mountains to find her sister, leaving Hans in charge of the kingdom.

Anna hired a man called Kristoff to be her guide. Kristoff had a reindeer called Sven. Soon, a magical snowman called Olaf joined them! He was the snowman that Elsa had made when she and Anna were children. Olaf led his new friends up the mountain to the magnificent ice palace that Elsa had created.

Elsa was enjoying her
time alone. Now that she
no longer had to worry about
hurting anyone, she was free to
be herself. She created many beautiful
things out of ice and snow.

'Whoa!' said Anna in awe as they reached the top of
the mountain. The palace was amazing!

When they found Elsa, Anna explained that the kingdom was
freezing, and no-one knew what to do. She begged Elsa to come
home and help. But Elsa was afraid.

'You should go, Anna,' she warned. 'I'm too dangerous.'

The more Anna tried to persuade Elsa, the more frightened Elsa
became. Finally, she accidentally cast a magic freezing spell on
Anna and made a giant snowman to chase her away.

Let's Subtract

Read the problem.
Write the difference.
The first one is done for you.

There are 3 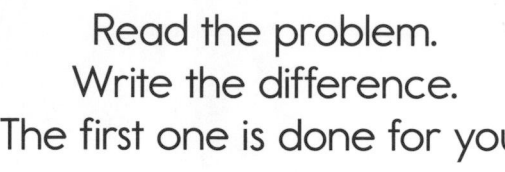.

2  melt away.
How many are left?

__3__ take away __2__ is __1__.

There are 4 ❄.

2 ❄ melt away.
How many are left?

___ take away ___ is ___.

There are 5 ❄.

3 ❄ melt away.
How many are left?

___ take away ___ is ___.

There are 6 ❄.

2 ❄ melt away.
How many are left?

___ take away ___ is ___.

There are 7 ❄.

3 ❄ melt away.
How many are left?

___ take away ___ is ___.

There are 9 ❄ .

2 ❄ melt away.

How many are left?

___ take away ___ is ___ .

There are 10 ❄ .

5 ❄ melt away.

How many are left?

___ take away ___ is ___ .

There are 11 ❄ .

6 ❄ melt away.

How many are left?

___ take away ___ is ___ .

There are 12 ❄ .

7 ❄ melt away.

How many are left?

___ take away ___ is ___ .

Write your own maths story.

There are ⬜ snowflakes.

⬜ snowflakes melt away.

How many are left?

⬜ take away ⬜ is ⬜ .

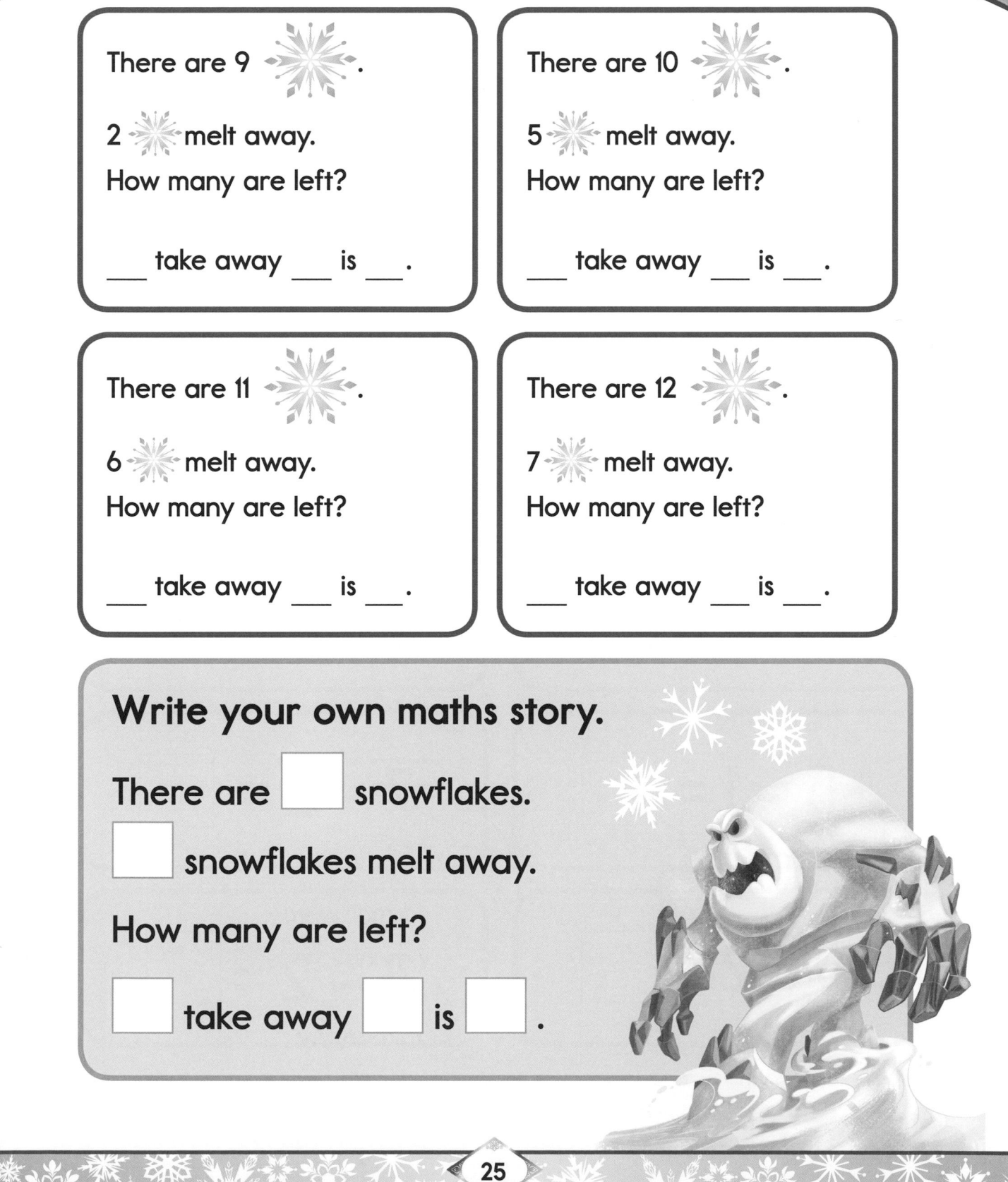

Let's Count
Back to Subtract

Count back to subtract. Use the number line to help.
Write the difference. The first one is done for you.

0 1 2 3 4 5 6 7 8 9 10 11 12

$$8 - 1 = \boxed{7}$$

$$9 - 1 = \square$$

$$10 - 1 = \square$$

$$8 - 2 = \square$$

$$9 - 2 = \square$$

$$5 - 1 = \square$$

$$7 - 2 = \square$$

$$6 - 2 = \square$$

$$4 - 2 = \square$$

Count back to subtract. Use the number line to help. Write the difference.

0 1 2 3 4 5 6 7 8 9 10 11 12

3 − 2 = ☐

4 − 1 = ☐

10 − 2 = ☐

5 − 2 = ☐

7 − 1 = ☐

6 − 1 = ☐

Let's Count
Back to Subtract

Count back to subtract. Use the number
line to help. Write the difference.

9 – 3 = ☐

11 – 1 = ☐

12 – 2 = ☐

8 – 3 = ☐

10 – 3 = ☐

11 – 2 = ☐

12 – 3 = ☐

11 – 3 = ☐

8 – 2 = ☐

10 – 2 = ☐

Let's Learn Fact Families

Numbers in a fact family are related. Complete each fact family.
The first one is done for you. Use the dice to help.

4 + 3 = _7_   _7_ − 3 = 4
3 + 4 = _7_   _7_ − 4 = 3

6 + 5 = ___   11 − ___ = 5
___ + 6 = 11   ___ − 5 = 6

___ + 6 = ___   ___ − ___ = 6
___ + 4 = 10   ___ − ___ = 4

___ + ___ = ___   ___ − ___ = ___
___ + ___ = ___   ___ − ___ = ___

Let's Learn Fact Families

Complete each fact family.
Use the dice to help.

9 + 3 = ___   12 − ___ = 3

___ + 9 = 12   ___ − 3 = 9

7 + 4 = ___   11 − ___ = 4

___ + 7 = 11   ___ − 4 = 7

___ + 5 = ___   ___ − ___ = 5

___ + 7 = 12   ___ − ___ = 7

___ + ___ = ___   ___ − ___ = ___

___ + ___ = ___   ___ − ___ = ___

Let's Add and Subtract

Add or subtract. Write the answers.
The first ones are done for you.

add 2

+2

IN	OUT
4	6
2	
8	
5	

take away 1

−1

IN	OUT
6	5
3	
9	
11	

Let's Subtract
Larger Numbers

Write the difference.
The first one is done for you.

19 – 6 = 13

18 – 2 = ☐

16 – 2 = ☐

20 – 5 = ☐

17 – 3 = ☐

16 – 4 = ☐

14 – 1 = ☐

15 – 5 = ☐

6 10

14 20

22 26 30

34 38 40

42 46 50

10 15

25 35

45

20 30

50 70

90

© Disney

Only an act of true love will thaw a freezing heart

ELSA

Anna

© Disney

ELSA

FROZEN

© Disney

Let's Add and Subtract Tens

Write the answer.
The first one is done for you.

30 + 10 = 40

40 – 30 = ☐

60 + 20 = ☐

80 – 60 = ☐

40 + 50 = ☐

90 – 40 = ☐

50 + 30 = ☐

80 – 30 = ☐

Let's Race

Solve the problems to escape the giant snowman.
Record your time and the number of correct answers.
On your marks, get set, go!

7 + 2 =	8 – 5 =	6 – 5 =	9 + 2 =
15 – 3 =	6 – 4 =	2 + 8 =	10 – 3 =
18 – 7 =	7 + 1 =	10 – 10 =	4 + 5 =
5 + 4 =	30 + 20 =	5 + 6 =	8 + 4 =
5 – 3 =	3 + 6 =	8 – 0 =	9 – 7 =
4 – 2 =	2 + 2 =	80 – 40 =	1 + 3 =

Time to Complete: _____

Total Answers: _____

Total Correct: _____

Keep it up!
See if you can beat your score.
On your marks, get set, go!

6 + 3 =	12 – 4 =	10 – 9 =	8 + 3 =
3 + 8 =	12 – 5 =	16 – 3 =	11 – 6 =
7 + 4 =	8 – 1 =	30 + 60 =	4 + 0 =
5 + 3 =	9 – 2 =	70 – 30 =	8 + 1 =
12 – 3 =	3 + 7 =	8 – 7 =	11 – 4 =
10 – 6 =	10 – 2 =	11 – 7 =	7 – 1 =

Time to Complete: _____

Total Answers: _____

Total Correct: _____

Kristoff and Anna ran away to safety, but something was wrong. Anna's hair was turning white.

'It's because she struck you with her powers, isn't it?' Kristoff asked, concerned. 'We need to go and see my friends,' he said. 'They can help.'

Kristoff led Anna, Olaf and Sven into the valley where his friends, the trolls, lived. The old troll said that Elsa had put ice in Anna's heart, which would freeze her solid. But there was still hope. 'An act of true love can thaw a frozen heart,' he explained.

Quickly, Kristoff and Anna headed back to Arendelle. Surely Prince Hans could break the spell with a true love's kiss.

But when Anna returned to Arendelle and found Hans, he refused to kiss her!

Instead, he left Anna alone in the cold room and locked Elsa in a dungeon. He didn't care what happened to Anna or Elsa, he just wanted to take over the kingdom.

Anna was about to give up, but then Olaf found her. He helped her find the strength to go back to Kristoff. Perhaps Kristoff could break the spell!

Let's Count to Add and Subtract

1	2	3	4	5
6	7	8	9	10
11	12	13	14	15
16	17	18	19	20
21	22	23	24	25
26	27	28	29	30
31	32	33	34	35
36	37	38	39	40
41	42	43	44	45
46	47	48	49	50

Start at 5. Count up 3. Write the number.   __8__

Start at 15. Count up 5. Write the number.   ____

Start at 25. Count back 2. Write the number.   ____

Start at 30. Count back 4. Write the number.   ____

Let's Count in 2s

Count in 2s.
Use your stickers to fill in the missing numbers.

 2, 4, ☐, 8, ☐

 12, ☐, 16, 18, ☐

 ☐, 24, ☐, 28, ☐

 32, ☐, 36, ☐, ☐

 ☐, 44, ☐, 48, ☐

Let's Count in 5s

Count in 5s.
Use your stickers to fill in the missing numbers.

START

5

20

30

40

50

FINISH

Let's Count in 10s

Count in 10s.
Use your stickers to fill in the missing numbers.

Let's Count
in 2s, 5s and 10s

1	2	3	4	5
6	7	8	9	10
11	12	13	14	15
16	17	18	19	20
21	22	23	24	25
26	27	28	29	30
31	32	33	34	35
36	37	38	39	40
41	42	43	44	45
46	47	48	49	50

Start at 2. Count in 2s to 10.
Write the numbers.

__2__, __4__, ____, ____, ____

Start at 5. Count in 5s to 25.
Write the numbers.

__5__, ____, ____, ____, ____

Start at 10. Count in 10s to 50.
Write the numbers.

__10__, ____, ____, ____, ____

Let's Add Doubles

Add the doubles. Write the sum.

2 + 2 = ☐

4 + 4 = ☐

5 + 5 = ☐

3 + 3 = ☐

10 + 10 = ☐

9 + 9 = ☐

Try this:

8 + 8 = ☐   80 + 80 = ☐

Let's Add
Doubles Plus 1

Write the sum. Use the doubles to help.

7 + 7 = ☐

7 + 8 = ☐

5 + 5 = ☐

5 + 6 = ☐

6 + 6 = ☐

6 + 7 = ☐

8 + 8 = ☐

8 + 9 = ☐

4 + 5 = ☐

2 + 3 = ☐

7 + 6 = ☐

9 + 8 = ☐

Let's Add 10

Use the counters to help you add and write the missing numbers. The first one is done for you.

$8 + 3 = \underline{11}$

$1 + 10 = \underline{11}$

$9 + 4 = \underline{}$

$\underline{} + 10 = \underline{}$

$8 + 4 = \underline{}$

$\underline{} + 10 = \underline{}$

$6 + 7 = \underline{}$

$\underline{} + 10 = \underline{}$

Let's Race

Solve the problems to help Elsa escape the dungeon.
Record your time and the number of correct answers.
On your marks, get set, go!

7 + 7 =	8 + 9 =	5 + 6 =	6 + 9 =
8 + 8 =	3 + 4 =	8 + 4 =	11 + 4 =
6 + 8 =	9 + 4 =	7 + 6 =	3 + 3 =
8 + 7 =	11 + 3 =	10 + 6 =	12 + 5 =
4 + 4 =	9 + 7 =	7 + 8 =	6 + 6 =
5 + 5 =	9 + 6 =	10 + 4 =	6 + 1 =

Time to Complete: _____

Total Answers: _____

Total Correct: _____

Keep it up!
See if you can beat your score.
On your marks, get set, go!

6 + 3 =	12 – 4 =	10 – 9 =	8 + 3 =
3 + 8 =	5 – 2 =	6 + 6 =	11 – 6 =
7 + 4 =	8 – 1 =	11 – 11 =	4 + 0 =
5 + 3 =	9 – 2 =	5 + 5 =	8 + 1 =
12 – 3 =	3 + 7 =	8 – 7 =	11 – 4 =
10 – 6 =	10 – 2 =	11 – 7 =	12 – 8 =

Time to Complete: _____

Total Answers: _____

Total Correct: _____

Let's Learn
Subtraction Facts

Subtract. Write the difference.

11 – 5 = ☐

13 – 8 = ☐

12 – 12 = ☐

16 – 7 = ☐

14 – 5 = ☐

15 – 3 = ☐

17 – 6 = ☐

Let's Match Facts

Subtract.
Write the addition fact that helps.
The first one is done for you.

8 – 6 = [2]

6 + [2] = 8

12 – 4 = [ ]

4 + [ ] = 12

9 – 3 = [ ]

3 + [ ] = 9

10 – 6 = [ ]

6 + [ ] = 10

11 – 7 = [ ]

7 + [ ] = 11

Let's Match Facts

Subtract.
Write the addition fact that helps.
The first one is done for you.

11 − 6 = 5

6 + 5 = 11

15 − 8 = ☐

8 + ☐ = 15

14 − 6 = ☐

6 + ☐ = 14

13 − 4 = ☐

4 + ☐ = 13

Let's Match
Larger Facts

Write the addition and subtraction facts.
The first one is done for you

3 + 6 = $\boxed{9}$

30 + 60 = $\boxed{90}$

7 − 2 = ☐

70 − 20 = ☐

8 + 2 = ☐

80 + 20 = ☐

9 − 5 = ☐

90 − 50 = ☐

10 + 70 = ☐

60 − 50 = ☐

Let's Race

Help Kristoff reach Anna before she freezes.
Record your time and the number of correct answers.
On your marks, get set, go!

11 – 7 =	13 – 9 =	9 – 8 =	10 – 6 =
14 – 1 =	100 – 50 =	8 – 7 =	11 – 4 =
9 – 6 =	9 – 4 =	7 – 6 =	12 – 3 =
9 – 7 =	15 – 2 =	10 – 4 =	12 – 2 =
8 – 6 =	20 + 60 =	11 – 2 =	9 – 5 =
14 – 3 =	11 – 6 =	16 – 2 =	10 – 2 =

Time to Complete: _____

Total Answers: _____

Total Correct: _____

Keep it up!
See if you can beat your score.
On your marks, get set, go!

30 + 30 =	15 – 3 =	10 – 8 =	12 – 5 =
13 – 3 =	15 – 1 =	13 – 2 =	16 – 0 =
13 – 1 =	11 – 3 =	12 – 1 =	11 – 5 =
12 – 4 =	14 – 2 =	8 – 8 =	14 – 4 =
16 – 1 =	40 + 30 =	90 – 70 =	8 – 5 =
10 – 3 =	9 – 4 =	80 – 40 =	19 – 4 =

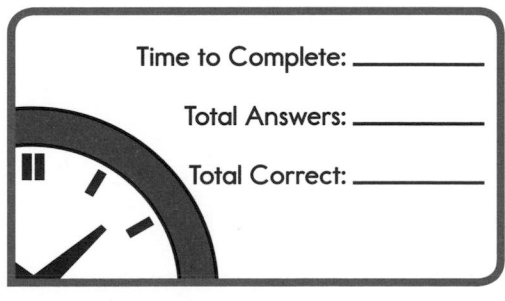

Time to Complete: _____

Total Answers: _____

Total Correct: _____

Let's Match Facts

Subtract.
Write the addition fact that helps.
The first one is done for you.

16 − 7 = $\boxed{9}$

7 + $\boxed{9}$ = 16

18 − 9 = $\boxed{}$

9 + $\boxed{}$ = 18

12 − 5 = $\boxed{}$

5 + $\boxed{}$ = 12

17 − 9 = $\boxed{}$

9 + $\boxed{}$ = 17

15 − 7 = $\boxed{}$

7 + $\boxed{}$ = 15

Let's Solve Word Problems

Read the problem.
Write the number sentence.
The first one is done for you.

Olaf has 1 carrot.

Kristoff has 6 more.

How many carrots in total?

$$\underline{1} + \underline{6} = \underline{7}$$

Kristoff makes 10 snowballs.

Hans makes 6 more.

How many snowballs in total?

$$\underline{} + \underline{} = \underline{}$$

Anna has 10 dresses.

3 get wet in the snow.

How many are left?

$$\underline{} - \underline{} = \underline{}$$

Elsa makes 8 ice sculptures.

4 sculptures melt.

How many are left?

$$\underline{} - \underline{} = \underline{}$$

Sven has 14 apples.

He eats 6 apples.

How many are left?

$$\underline{} - \underline{} = \underline{}$$

Let's Add and Subtract

Add or subtract to find the answers.
The first ones are done for you.

add 3

IN	OUT
11	14
10	
12	
15	

take away 3

IN	OUT
14	11
12	
11	
18	

Let's Use a Graph

Look at the graph.
Answer the questions. Count the cells to help.

8				
7				
6				
5				
4				
3				
2				
1				

How many more cells does [Elsa] have than [Anna]? ☐

How many fewer cells does [Olaf] have than [Kristoff]? ☐

How many cells does [Kristoff] and [Olaf] have in all? ☐

Let's Race

Solve the problems.
Record your time and the number of correct answers.
On your marks, get set, go!

14 + 2 =	15 – 2 =	12 – 5 =	9 + 9 =
10 + 5 =	13 – 1 =	14 + 3 =	17 – 3 =
8 + 8 =	12 – 3 =	13 – 0 =	12 + 1 =
10 + 4 =	16 – 2 =	11 + 2 =	8 + 5 =
9 – 7 =	10 + 6 =	13 – 5 =	14 – 4 =
17 – 0 =	12 + 3 =	12 – 4 =	7 + 8 =

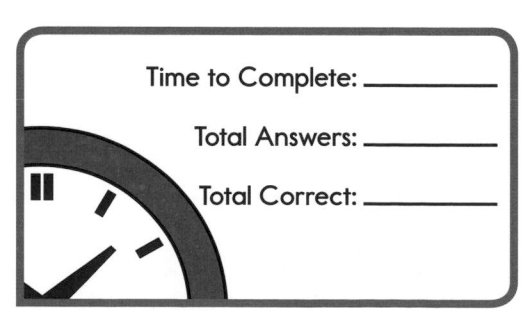

Time to Complete: _____

Total Answers: _____

Total Correct: _____

Keep it up!
See if you can beat your score.
On your marks, get set, go!

9 + 5 =	12 – 3 =	14 – 3 =	7 + 1 =
10 + 3 =	16 – 2 =	15 + 1 =	12 – 6 =
9 + 6 =	11 – 3 =	15 – 15 =	8 + 7 =
6 + 8 =	15 – 5 =	14 + 0 =	9 + 9 =
17 – 7 =	5 + 6 =	11 – 7 =	11 – 4 =
13 – 6 =	14 + 4 =	16 – 7 =	10 + 2 =

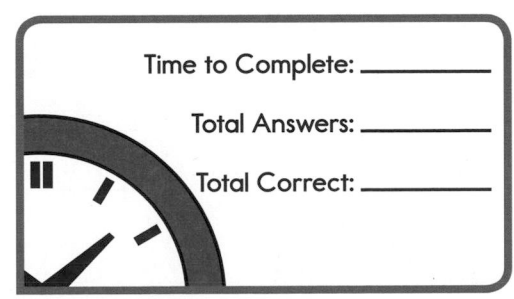

Time to Complete: _____

Total Answers: _____

Total Correct: _____

Let's Read

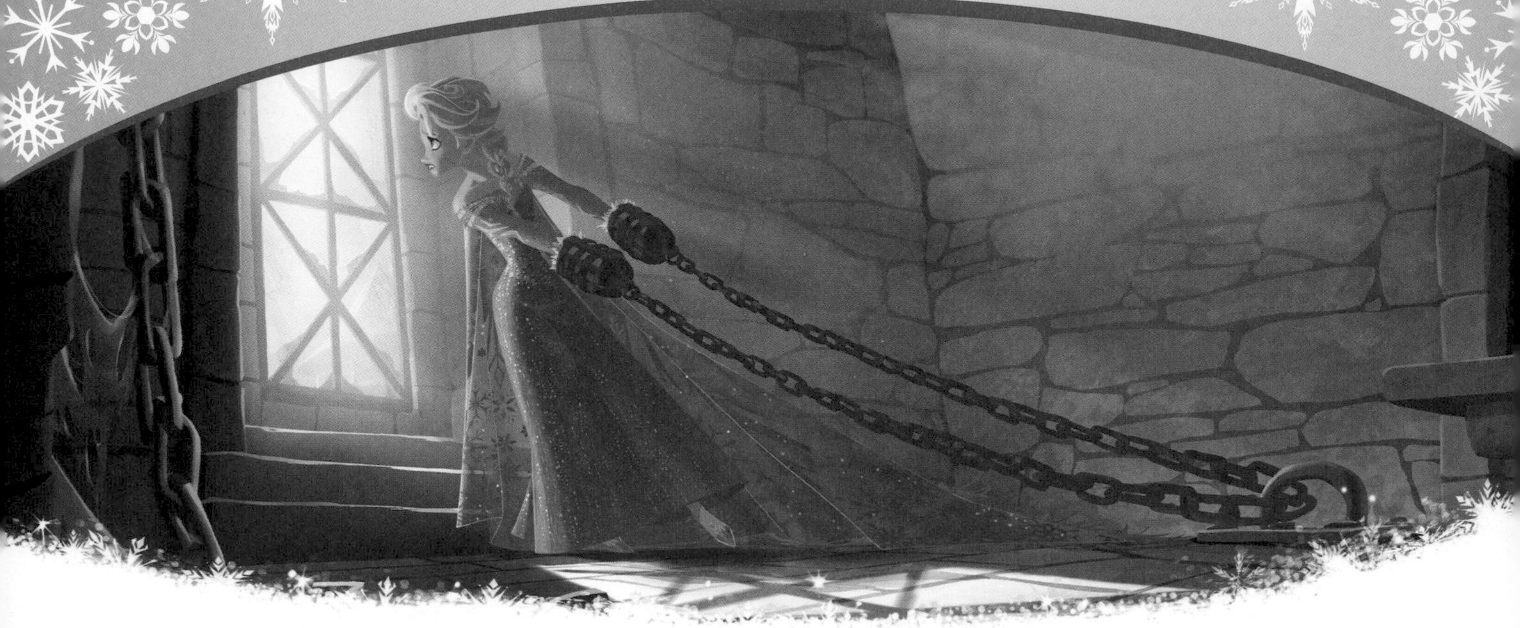

In the dungeon, all Elsa could think about was getting away. Finally, she managed to freeze the whole dungeon and escape!

Olaf helped Anna outside and she spotted Kristoff. If she could reach him in time, she would be saved! But then she saw something else – Hans had caught up with Elsa and was about to attack her!

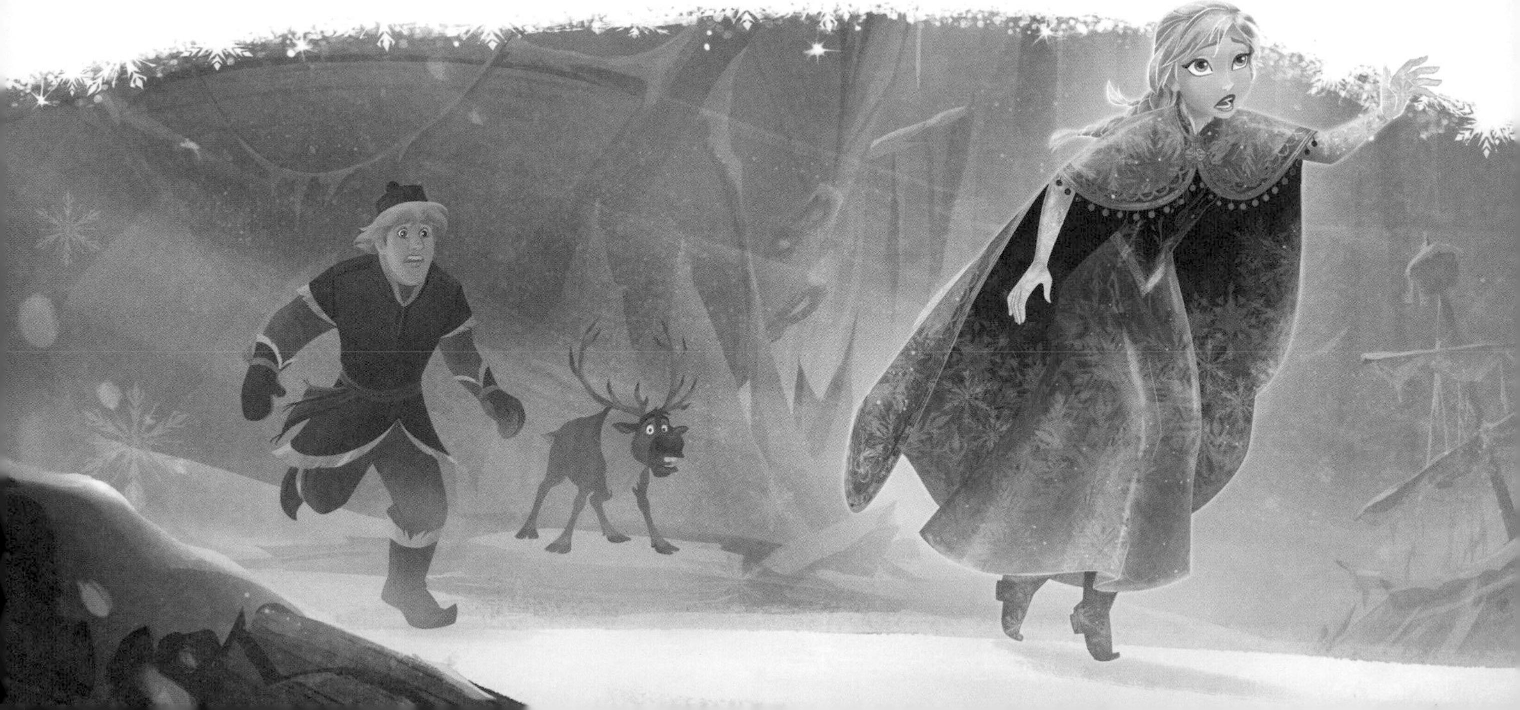

When Anna saw Hans, she threw herself in front of Elsa. Hans's sword came down just as Anna's body froze to solid ice. With a loud CLANK, the blade shattered.

Anna had saved her sister! And it was an act of true love – true love between two sisters. The spell broke and the ice melted. Anna was restored!

As for Elsa, she became queen again – a good queen who had learned from her sister that love was the key to controlling her powers. She even created an ice-skating rink in the castle. Everyone had a wonderful time skating!

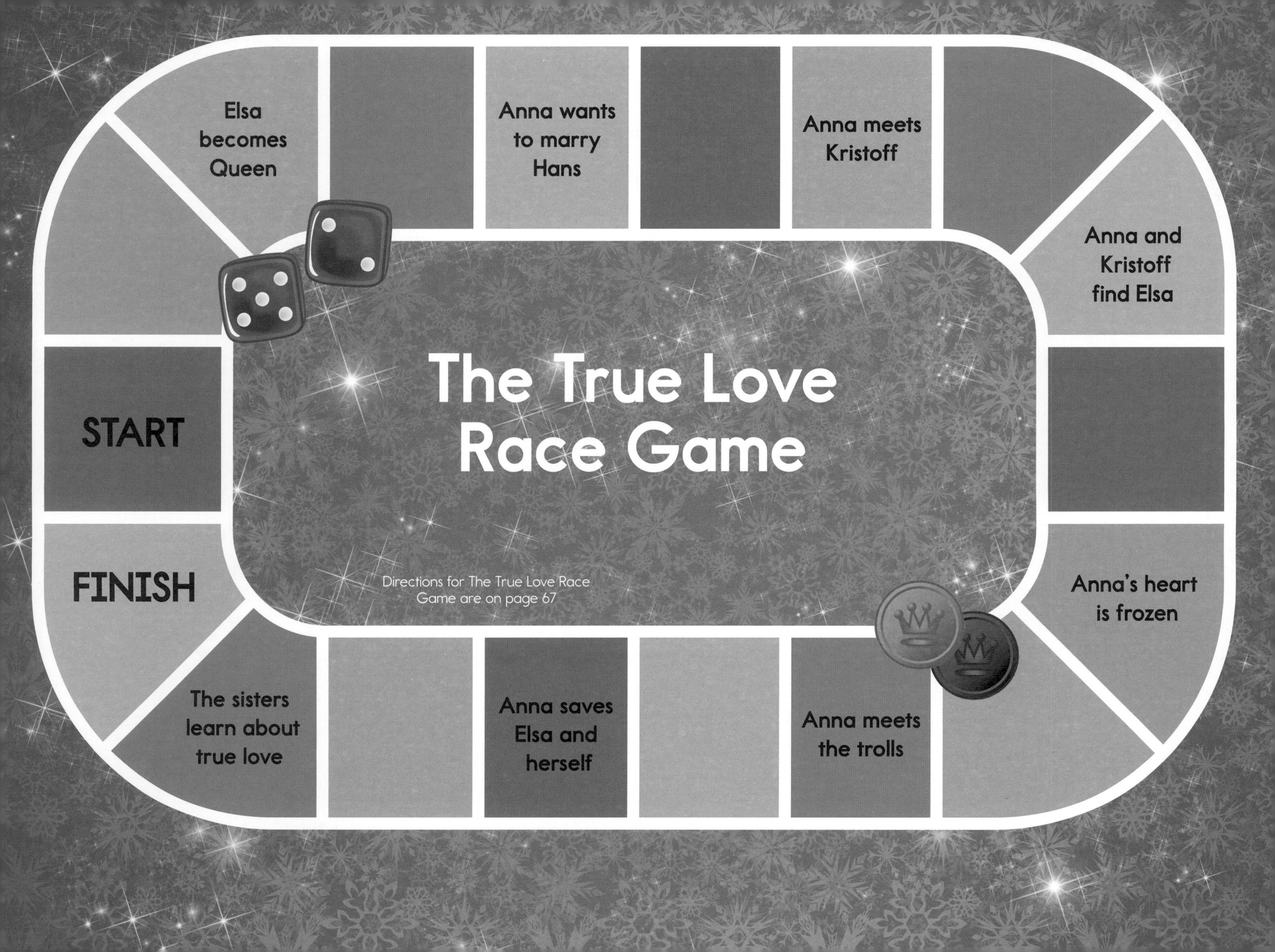

The True Love Race Game

Directions for The True Love Race Game are on page 67

START

FINISH

Elsa becomes Queen

Anna wants to marry Hans

Anna meets Kristoff

Anna and Kristoff find Elsa

Anna's heart is frozen

Anna meets the trolls

Anna saves Elsa and herself

The sisters learn about true love

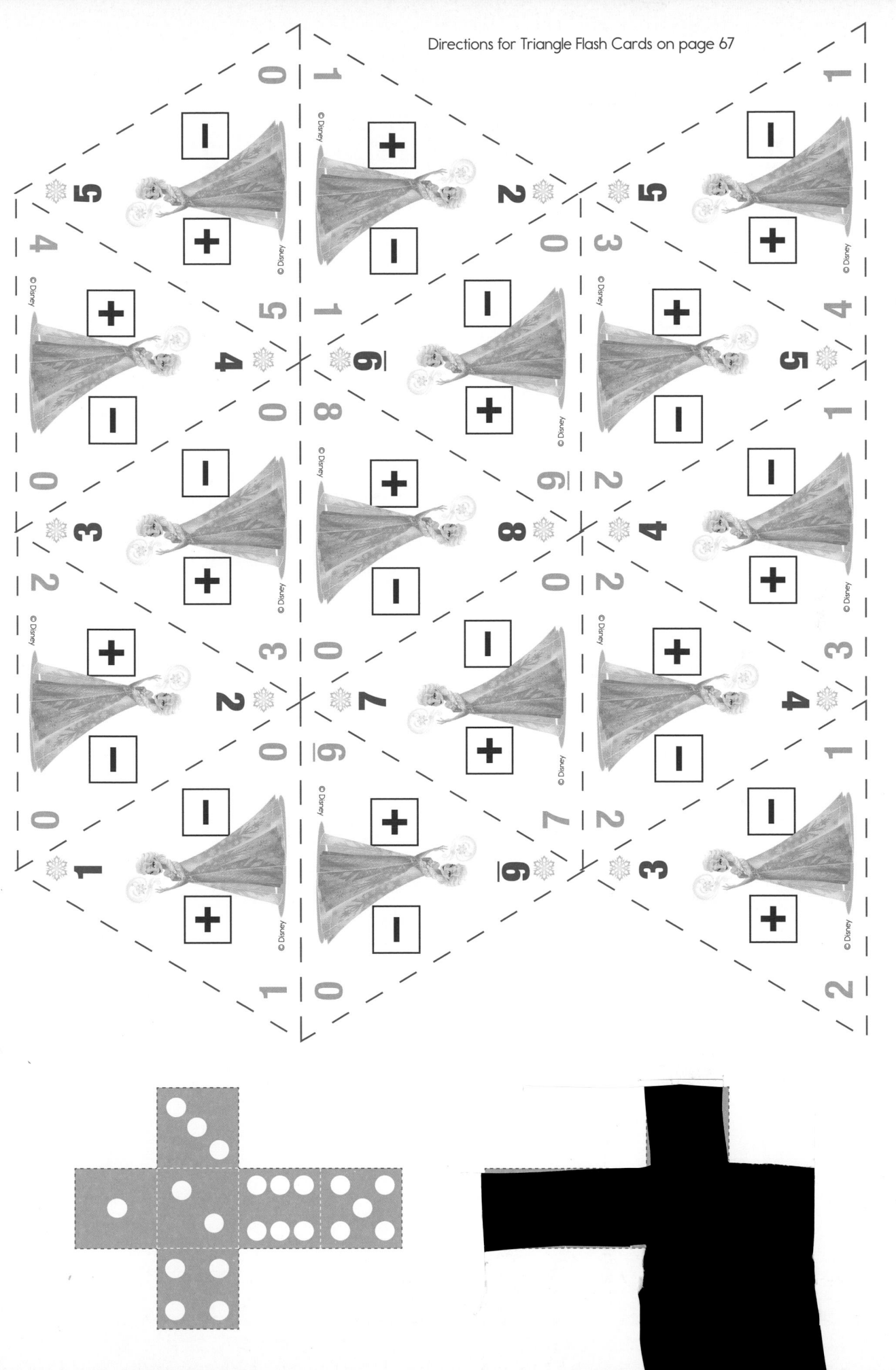

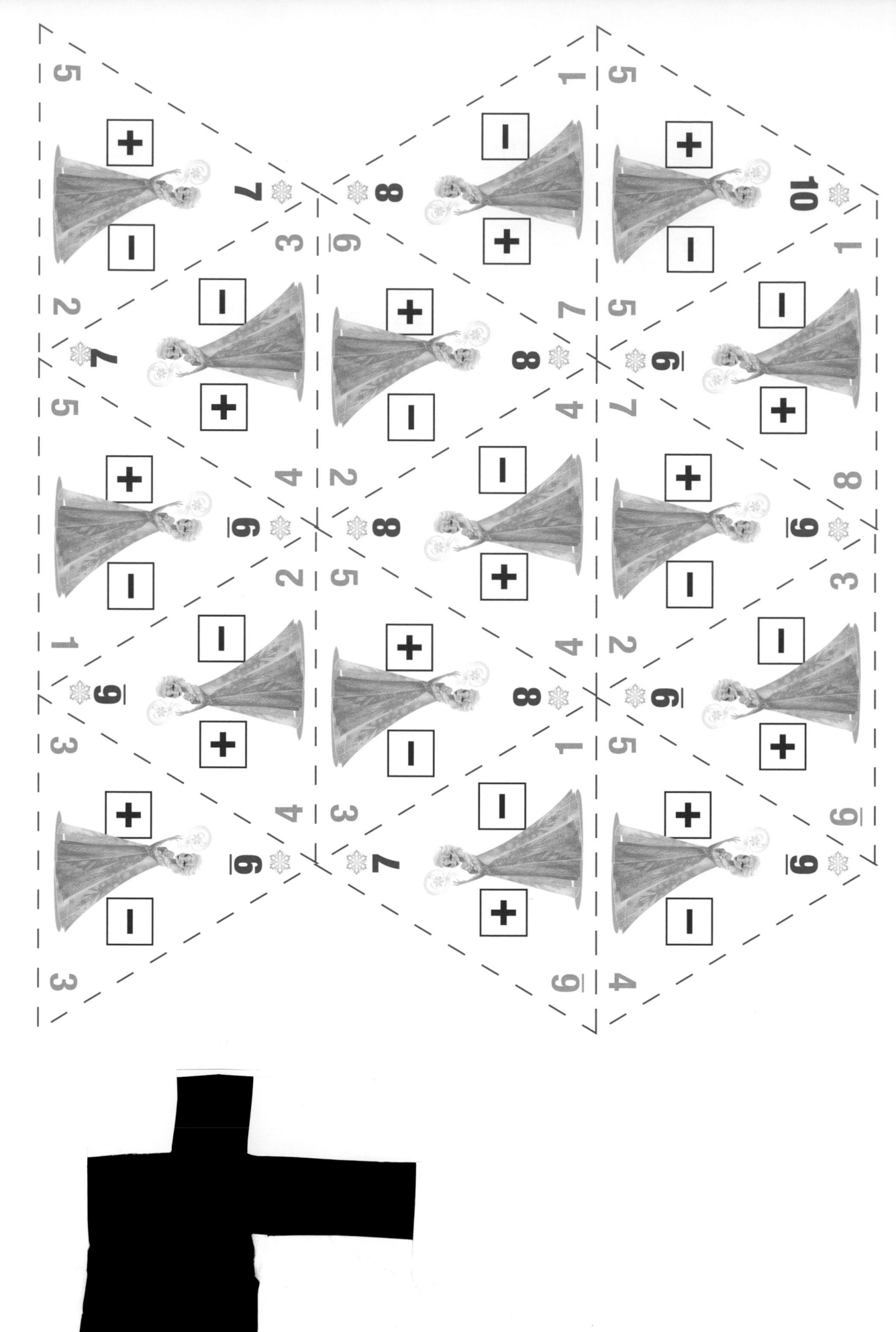

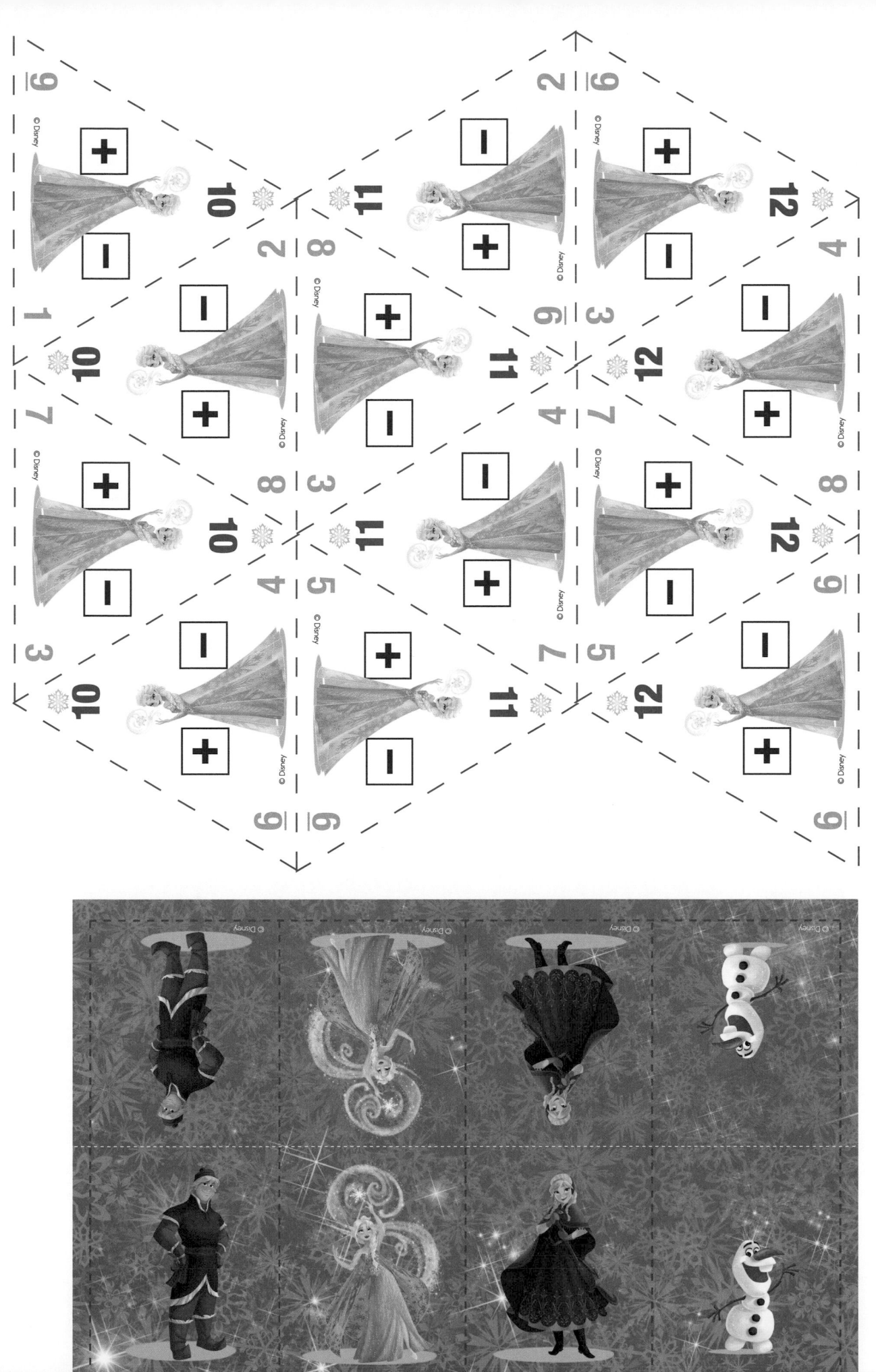

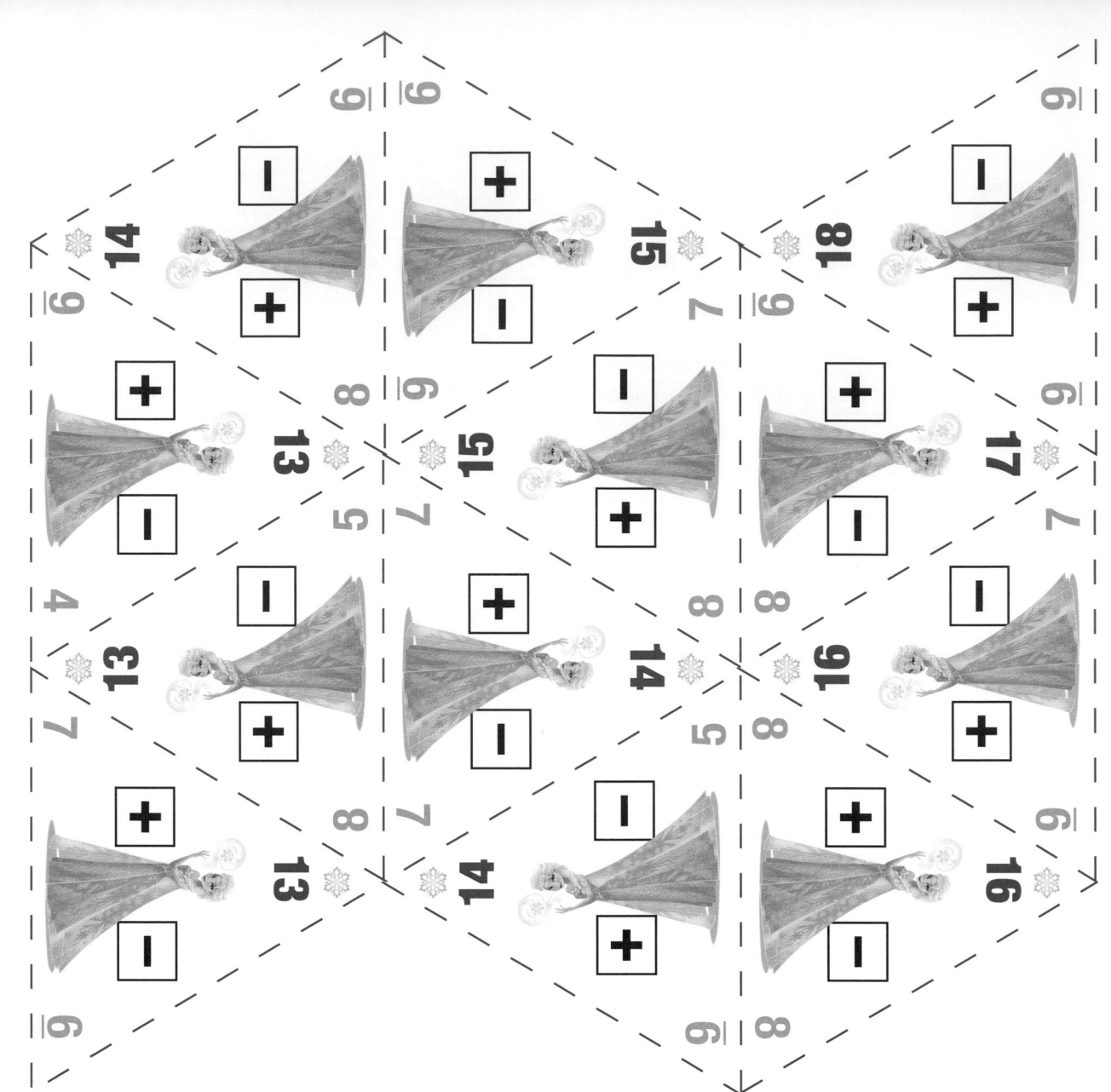

The True Love Race Game
A game for two to four players

Set Up

• Ask an adult to help you carefully cut around the pink lines on the game pieces at the bottom of page 65. Fold each game piece in half so they stand upright.

• Carefully cut out the dice at the bottom of page 63. Make each die by following the directions below:

1. Fold each die on the dotted lines.

2. Tape the edges to make a cube.

3. You are ready to roll!

How To Play

• Each player chooses a game piece and places it on the **START** space.

• Decide which player will go first.

• Players take turns rolling the dice. For each turn, players:
  – add the numbers together
  – subtract 2 from the sum
  – move ahead that many spaces in a clockwise direction

• The first player to reach the **FINISH** space is the winner!

Triangle Flash Cards

Disney's Triangle Flash Cards are great for maths facts, review and practice. The three numbers on each card create a set of maths facts. You can make both addition AND subtraction facts.

$$2 + 3 = 5$$
$$3 + 2 = 5$$
$$5 - 3 = 2$$
$$5 - 2 = 3$$

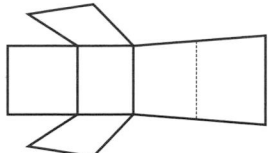

• Make the Triangle Flash Cards found on pages 63 and 65 by asking an adult to help you cut along the pink dotted lines.

• For addition practice, cover the red number at the top by the snowflake. This is the sum. Look at the two blue numbers on the card to solve the maths fact. Uncover the hidden number to check.

$$2 + 3 = 5$$

• For subtraction practice, cover one blue number. Look at the two numbers on the card to solve the maths fact. Uncover the hidden number to check.

$$5 - 3 = 2$$

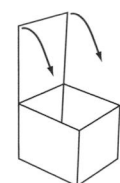

• Quickly recall individual facts aloud. For more fact practice, tell the related subtraction or addition fact for both numbers.

$$2 + 3 = 5 \qquad 5 - 3 = 2$$
$$3 + 2 = 5 \qquad 5 - 2 = 3$$

• One more challenge: write the fact family for each triangle flash card. These are the four related addition and subtraction facts. See pages 29 and 30 for examples.

Keep the practice fast and fun!

Answers

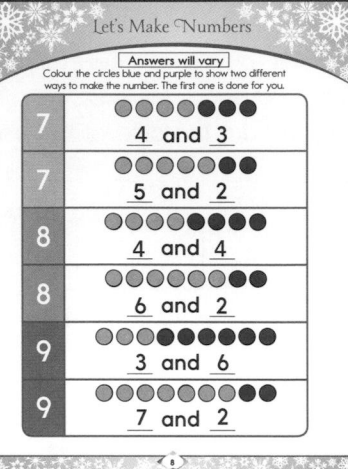

7	4 and 3
7	5 and 2
8	4 and 4
8	6 and 2
9	3 and 6
9	7 and 2

Answers will vary

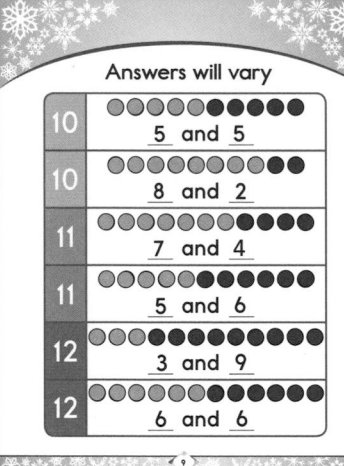

10	5 and 5
10	8 and 2
11	7 and 4
11	5 and 6
12	3 and 9
12	6 and 6

Let's Add

Read the problem.
Write the answer.
The first one is done for you.

There are 2
Elsa gets 2 more.
How many in total?
2 and 2 more is 4.

There are 5
Elsa gets 1 more.
How many in total?
5 and 1 more is 6.

There are 4
Olaf gets 2 more.
How many in total?
4 and 2 more is 6.

There are 6
Anna gets 3 more.
How many in total?
6 and 3 more is 9.

There are 7
Hans gets 2 more.
How many in total?
7 and 2 more is 9.

Let's Add

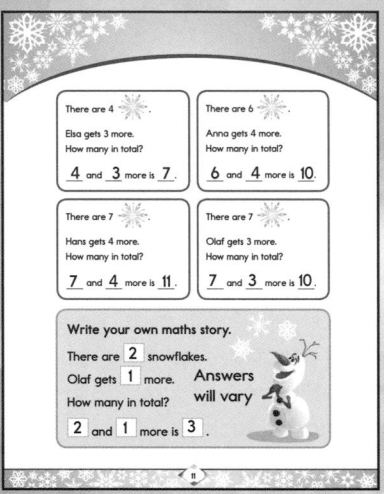

There are 4
Elsa gets 3 more.
How many in total?
4 and 3 more is 7.

There are 6
Anna gets 4 more.
How many in total?
6 and 4 more is 10.

There are 7
Hans gets 4 more.
How many in total?
7 and 4 more is 11.

There are 7
Olaf gets 3 more.
How many in total?
7 and 3 more is 10.

Write your own maths story.

There are 2 snowflakes.
Olaf gets 1 more.
How many in total?
2 and 1 more is 3.

Answers will vary

Let's Count On to Add

Count on to add. Use the number line to help.
Write the sum.
The first one is done for you.

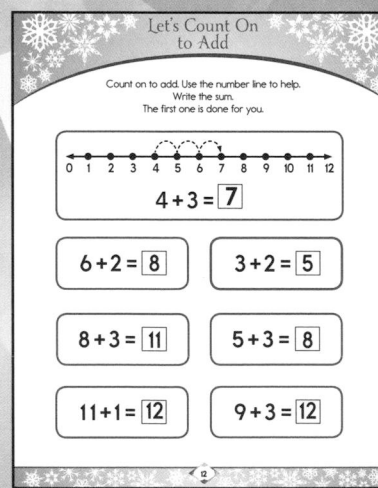

0 1 2 3 4 5 6 7 8 9 10 11 12

4 + 3 = 7

6 + 2 = 8   3 + 2 = 5

8 + 3 = 11   5 + 3 = 8

11 + 1 = 12   9 + 3 = 12

Let's Count On to Add

Count on to add. Use the number line to help.
Write the sum.

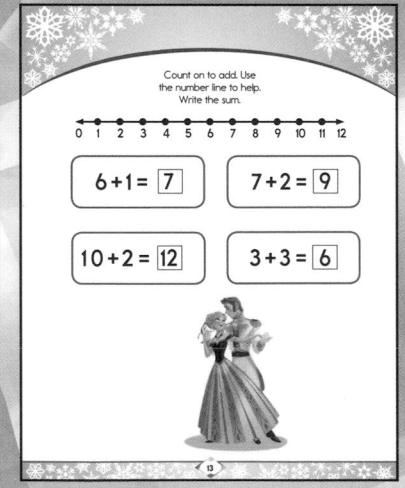

0 1 2 3 4 5 6 7 8 9 10 11 12

6 + 1 = 7   7 + 2 = 9

10 + 2 = 12   3 + 3 = 6

Let's Rearrange Number Sentences

Count the numbers on the dice. Write the sum.
Now rearrange the number sentence. The first one is done for you.

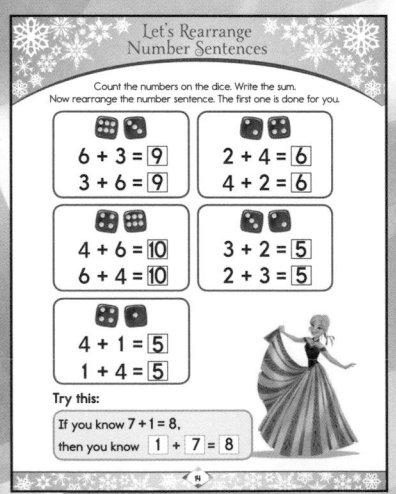

6 + 3 = 9
3 + 6 = 9

2 + 4 = 6
4 + 2 = 6

4 + 6 = 10
6 + 4 = 10

3 + 2 = 5
2 + 3 = 5

4 + 1 = 5
1 + 4 = 5

Try this:

If you know 7 + 1 = 8,
then you know 1 + 7 = 8

Answers

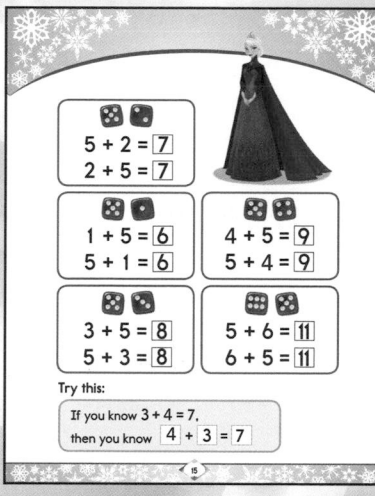

5 + 2 = 7
2 + 5 = 7

1 + 5 = 6
5 + 1 = 6

4 + 5 = 9
5 + 4 = 9

3 + 5 = 8
5 + 3 = 8

5 + 6 = 11
6 + 5 = 11

Try this:
If you know 3 + 4 = 7,
then you know 4 + 3 = 7

15

Let's Add 5

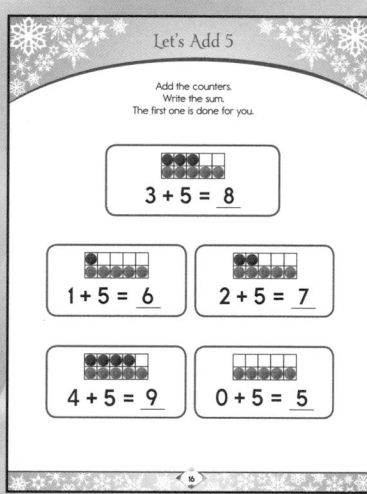

Add the counters.
Write the sum.
The first one is done for you.

3 + 5 = 8

1 + 5 = 6
2 + 5 = 7

4 + 5 = 9
0 + 5 = 5

16

Let's Colour

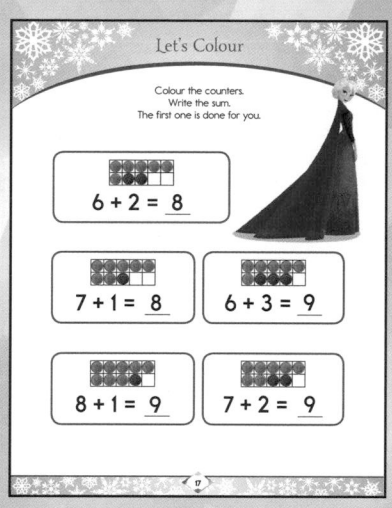

Colour the counters.
Write the sum.
The first one is done for you.

6 + 2 = 8

7 + 1 = 8
6 + 3 = 9

8 + 1 = 9
7 + 2 = 9

17

Let's Add Larger Numbers

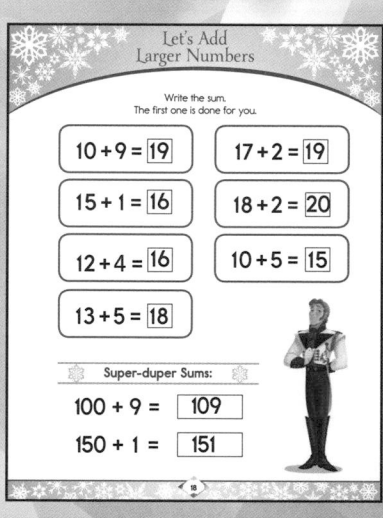

Write the sum.
The first one is done for you.

10 + 9 = 19
17 + 2 = 19
15 + 1 = 16
18 + 2 = 20
12 + 4 = 16
10 + 5 = 15
13 + 5 = 18

Super-duper Sums:
100 + 9 = 109
150 + 1 = 151

18

Let's Add Three Numbers

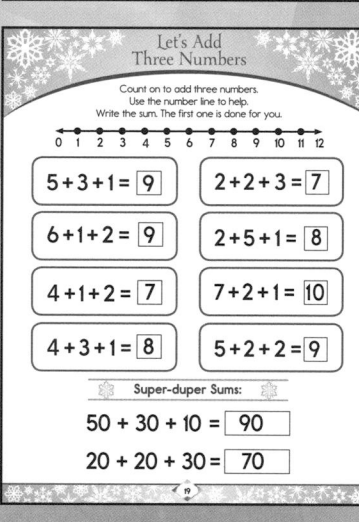

Count on to add three numbers.
Use the number line to help.
Write the sum. The first one is done for you.

0 1 2 3 4 5 6 7 8 9 10 11 12

5 + 3 + 1 = 9
2 + 2 + 3 = 7
6 + 1 + 2 = 9
2 + 5 + 1 = 8
4 + 1 + 2 = 7
7 + 2 + 1 = 10
4 + 3 + 1 = 8
5 + 2 + 2 = 9

Super-duper Sums:
50 + 30 + 10 = 90
20 + 20 + 30 = 70

19

Let's Race

Solve the problems to help Anna chase after Elsa.
Record your time and the number of correct answers.
On your marks, get set, go!

6 + 4 = 10	7 + 3 = 10	5 + 6 = 11	2 + 9 = 11
4 + 2 = 6	3 + 3 = 6	8 + 4 = 12	3 + 6 = 9
6 + 3 = 9	0 + 8 = 8	9 + 3 = 12	12 + 3 = 15
8 + 3 = 11	2 + 3 = 5	7 + 2 = 9	1 + 3 = 4
10 + 6 = 16	3 + 4 = 7	3 + 2 = 5	1 + 7 = 8
6 + 2 = 8	4 + 5 = 9	10 + 2 = 12	4+3+2=9

Time to Complete:
Total Answers:
Total Correct:

20

Keep it up!
See if you can beat your score.
On your mark, get set, go!

4 + 1 = 5	7 + 5 = 12	0 + 2 = 2	2 + 4 = 6
17 + 3 = 20	4 + 7 = 11	2 + 7 = 9	1 + 6 = 7
4 + 3 = 7	8 + 1 = 9	4 + 1 + 3 = 8	8 + 2 = 10
5 + 3 = 8	7 + 4 = 11	12 + 5 = 17	6+2+1=9
1 + 2 = 3	5 + 7 = 12	4 + 6 = 10	3+3+2=8
10 + 1 = 11	5 + 1 = 6	4 + 4 = 8	2 + 6 = 8

Time to Complete:
Total Answers:
Total Correct:

21

Let's Subtract

Read the problem.
Write the difference.
The first one is done for you.

There are 3. 2 melt away. How many are left?
3 take away 2 is 1.

There are 4. 2 melt away. How many are left?
4 take away 2 is 2.

There are 5. 3 melt away. How many are left?
5 take away 3 is 2.

There are 6. 2 melt away. How many are left?
6 take away 2 is 4.

There are 7. 3 melt away. How many are left?
7 take away 3 is 4.

24

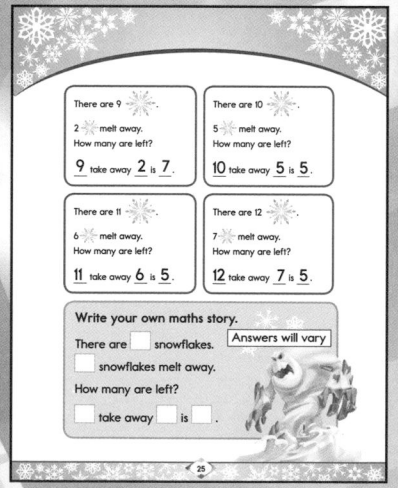

There are 9. 2 melt away. How many are left?
9 take away 2 is 7.

There are 10. 5 melt away. How many are left?
10 take away 5 is 5.

There are 11. 6 melt away. How many are left?
11 take away 6 is 5.

There are 12. 7 melt away. How many are left?
12 take away 7 is 5.

Write your own maths story.
There are [ ] snowflakes.   Answers will vary
[ ] snowflakes melt away.
How many are left?
[ ] take away [ ] is [ ].

25

Answers

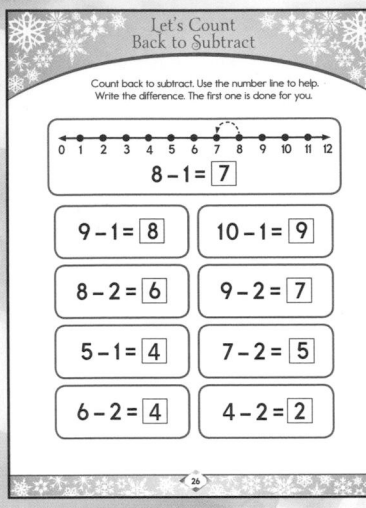

Let's Count Back to Subtract

Count back to subtract. Use the number line to help.
Write the difference. The first one is done for you.

0 1 2 3 4 5 6 7 8 9 10 11 12

8 – 1 = 7

9 – 1 = 8   10 – 1 = 9

8 – 2 = 6   9 – 2 = 7

5 – 1 = 4   7 – 2 = 5

6 – 2 = 4   4 – 2 = 2

26

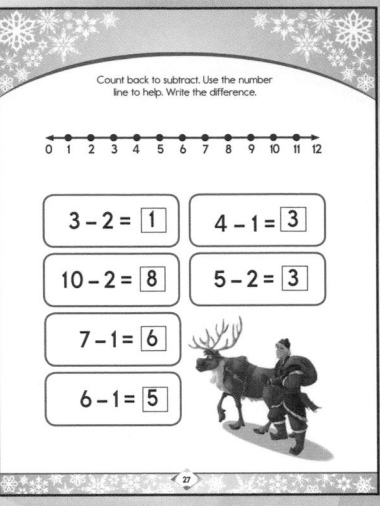

Let's Count Back to Subtract

Count back to subtract. Use the number line to help. Write the difference.

0 1 2 3 4 5 6 7 8 9 10 11 12

3 – 2 = 1   4 – 1 = 3

10 – 2 = 8   5 – 2 = 3

7 – 1 = 6

6 – 1 = 5

27

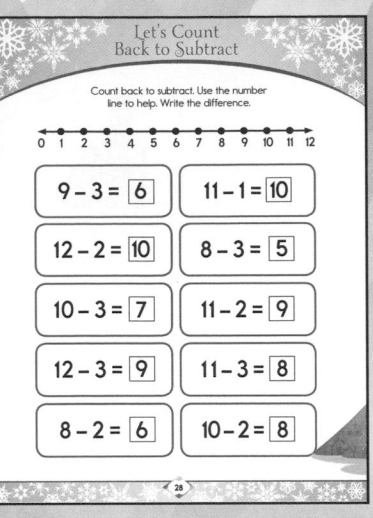

Let's Count Back to Subtract

Count back to subtract. Use the number line to help. Write the difference.

0 1 2 3 4 5 6 7 8 9 10 11 12

9 – 3 = 6   11 – 1 = 10

12 – 2 = 10   8 – 3 = 5

10 – 3 = 7   11 – 2 = 9

12 – 3 = 9   11 – 3 = 8

8 – 2 = 6   10 – 2 = 8

28

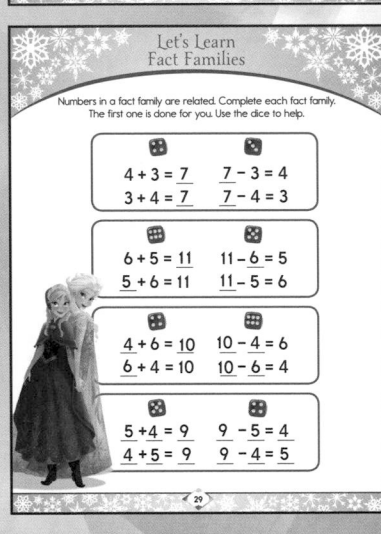

Let's Learn Fact Families

Numbers in a fact family are related. Complete each fact family.
The first one is done for you. Use the dice to help.

4 + 3 = 7   7 – 3 = 4
3 + 4 = 7   7 – 4 = 3

6 + 5 = 11   11 – 6 = 5
5 + 6 = 11   11 – 5 = 6

4 + 6 = 10   10 – 4 = 6
6 + 4 = 10   10 – 6 = 4

5 + 4 = 9   9 – 5 = 4
4 + 5 = 9   9 – 4 = 5

29

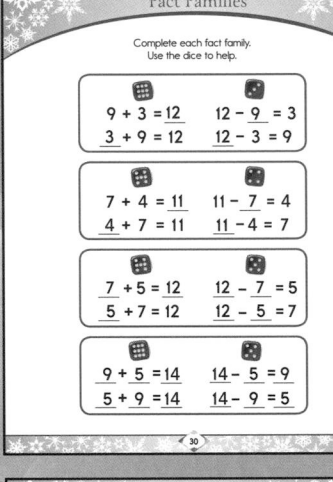

Let's Learn Fact Families

Complete each fact family.
Use the dice to help.

9 + 3 = 12   12 – 9 = 3
3 + 9 = 12   12 – 3 = 9

7 + 4 = 11   11 – 7 = 4
4 + 7 = 11   11 – 4 = 7

7 + 5 = 12   12 – 7 = 5
5 + 7 = 12   12 – 5 = 7

9 + 5 = 14   14 – 5 = 9
5 + 9 = 14   14 – 9 = 5

30

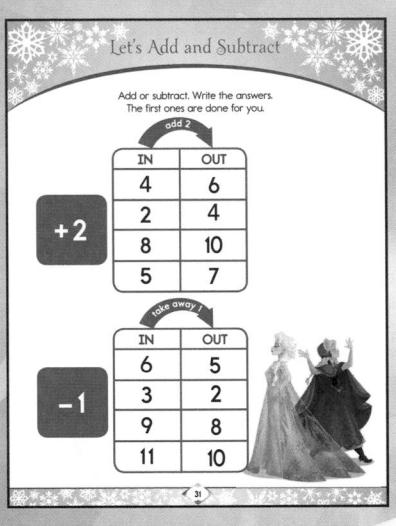

Let's Add and Subtract

Add or subtract. Write the answers.
The first ones are done for you.

add 2

IN	OUT
4	6
2	4
8	10
5	7

+2

take away 1

IN	OUT
6	5
3	2
9	8
11	10

–1

31

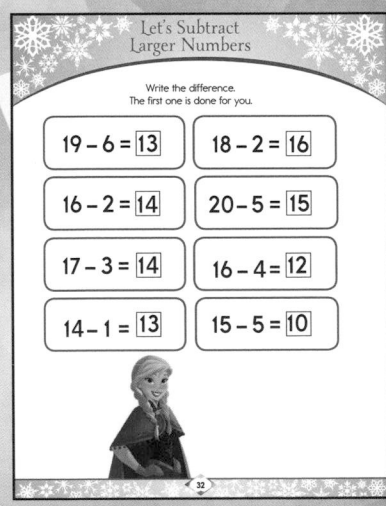

Let's Subtract Larger Numbers

Write the difference.
The first one is done for you.

19 – 6 = 13   18 – 2 = 16

16 – 2 = 14   20 – 5 = 15

17 – 3 = 14   16 – 4 = 12

14 – 1 = 13   15 – 5 = 10

32

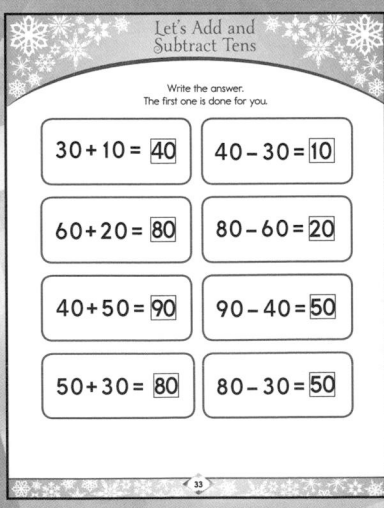

Let's Add and Subtract Tens

Write the answer.
The first one is done for you.

30 + 10 = 40   40 – 30 = 10

60 + 20 = 80   80 – 60 = 20

40 + 50 = 90   90 – 40 = 50

50 + 30 = 80   80 – 30 = 50

33

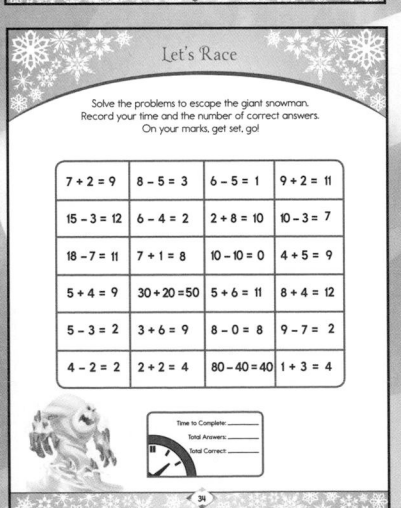

Let's Race

Solve the problems to escape the giant snowman.
Record your time and the number of correct answers.
On your marks, get set, go!

7 + 2 = 9	8 – 5 = 3	6 – 5 = 1	9 + 2 = 11
15 – 3 = 12	6 – 4 = 2	2 + 8 = 10	10 – 3 = 7
18 – 7 = 11	7 + 1 = 8	10 – 10 = 0	4 + 5 = 9
5 + 4 = 9	30 + 20 = 50	5 + 6 = 11	8 + 4 = 12
5 – 3 = 2	3 + 6 = 9	8 – 0 = 8	9 – 7 = 2
4 – 2 = 2	2 + 2 = 4	80 – 40 = 40	1 + 3 = 4

Time to Complete: _____
Total Answers: _____
Total Correct: _____

34

Answers

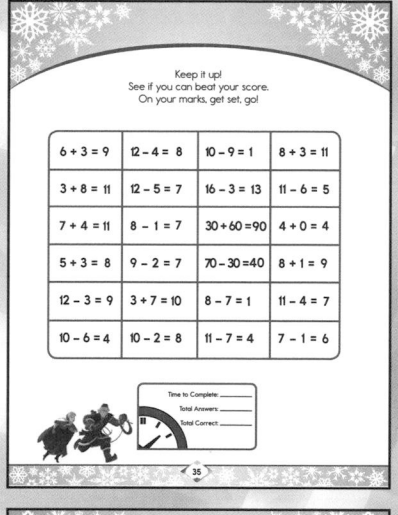

Keep it up!
See if you can beat your score.
On your marks, get set, go!

6 + 3 = 9	12 – 4 = 8	10 – 9 = 1	8 + 3 = 11
3 + 8 = 11	12 – 5 = 7	16 – 3 = 13	11 – 6 = 5
7 + 4 = 11	8 – 1 = 7	30 + 60 = 90	4 + 0 = 4
5 + 3 = 8	9 – 2 = 7	70 – 30 = 40	8 + 1 = 9
12 – 3 = 9	3 + 7 = 10	8 – 7 = 1	11 – 4 = 7
10 – 6 = 4	10 – 2 = 8	11 – 7 = 4	7 – 1 = 6

Time to Complete: _____
Total Answers: _____
Total Correct: _____

35

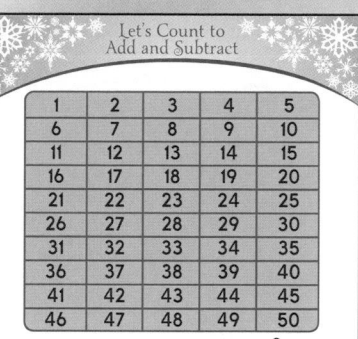

Let's Count to Add and Subtract

1	2	3	4	5
6	7	8	9	10
11	12	13	14	15
16	17	18	19	20
21	22	23	24	25
26	27	28	29	30
31	32	33	34	35
36	37	38	39	40
41	42	43	44	45
46	47	48	49	50

Start at 5. Count up 3. Write the number. __8__
Start at 15. Count up 5. Write the number. __20__
Start at 25. Count back 2. Write the number. __23__
Start at 30. Count back 4. Write the number. __26__

38

Let's Count in 2s

Count in 2s.
Use your stickers to fill in the missing numbers.

2, 4, 6, 8, 10

12, 14, 16, 18, 20

22, 24, 26, 28, 30

32, 34, 36, 38, 40

42, 44, 46, 48, 50

39

Let's Count in 5s

Count in 5s.
Use your stickers to fill in the missing numbers.

START 5 10 15 20 25 30 35 40 45 50 FINISH

40

Let's Count in 10s

Count in 10s.
Use your stickers to fill in the missing numbers.

START 10 20 30 40 50 60 70 80 90 100 FINISH

41

Let's Count in 2s, 5s and 10s

1	2	3	4	5
6	7	8	9	10
11	12	13	14	15
16	17	18	19	20
21	22	23	24	25
26	27	28	29	30
31	32	33	34	35
36	37	38	39	40
41	42	43	44	45
46	47	48	49	50

Start at 2. Count in 2s to 10.
Write the numbers. __2 4 6 8 10__

Start at 5. Count in 5s to 25.
Write the numbers. __5 10 15 20 25__

Start at 10. Count in 10s to 50.
Write the numbers. __10 20 30 40 50__

42

Let's Add Doubles

Add the doubles. Write the sum.

2 + 2 = 4   4 + 4 = 8

5 + 5 = 10   3 + 3 = 6

10 + 10 = 20
9 + 9 = 18

Try this:

8 + 8 = 16   80 + 80 = 160

43

Let's Add Doubles Plus 1

Write the sum. Use the doubles to help.

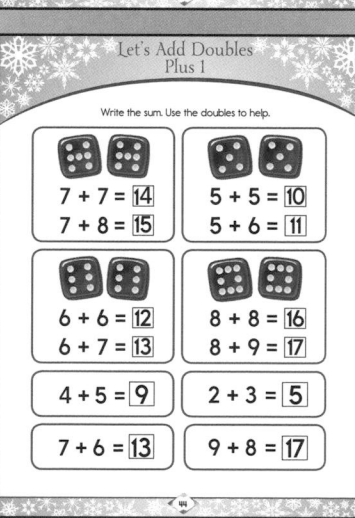

7 + 7 = 14   5 + 5 = 10
7 + 8 = 15   5 + 6 = 11

6 + 6 = 12   8 + 8 = 16
6 + 7 = 13   8 + 9 = 17

4 + 5 = 9   2 + 3 = 5

7 + 6 = 13   9 + 8 = 17

44

Let's Add 10

Use the counters to help you add and write the missing numbers. The first one is done for you.

8 + 3 = 11
1 + 10 = 11

9 + 4 = 13
3 + 10 = 13

8 + 4 = 12
2 + 10 = 12

6 + 7 = 13
3 + 10 = 13

45

Answers

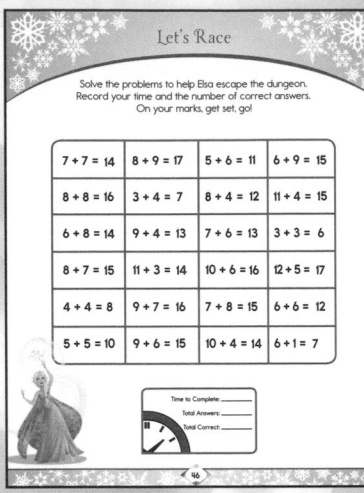

Let's Race

Solve the problems to help Elsa escape the dungeon.
Record your time and the number of correct answers.
On your marks, get set, go!

7 + 7 = 14	8 + 9 = 17	5 + 6 = 11	6 + 9 = 15
8 + 8 = 16	3 + 4 = 7	8 + 4 = 12	11 + 4 = 15
6 + 8 = 14	9 + 4 = 13	7 + 6 = 13	3 + 3 = 6
8 + 7 = 15	11 + 3 = 14	10 + 6 = 16	12 + 5 = 17
4 + 4 = 8	9 + 7 = 16	7 + 8 = 15	6 + 6 = 12
5 + 5 = 10	9 + 6 = 15	10 + 4 = 14	6 + 1 = 7

Time to Complete: _____
Total Answers: _____
Total Correct: _____

46

Keep it up!

See if you can beat your score.
On your marks, get set, go!

6 + 3 = 9	12 – 4 = 8	10 – 9 = 1	8 + 3 = 11
3 + 8 = 11	5 – 2 = 3	6 + 6 = 12	11 – 6 = 5
7 + 4 = 11	8 – 1 = 7	11 – 11 = 0	4 + 0 = 4
5 + 3 = 8	9 – 2 = 7	5 + 5 = 10	8 + 1 = 9
12 – 3 = 9	3 + 7 = 10	8 – 7 = 1	11 – 4 = 7
10 – 6 = 4	10 – 2 = 8	11 – 7 = 4	12 – 8 = 4

Time to Complete: _____
Total Answers: _____
Total Correct: _____

47

Let's Learn Subtraction Facts

Subtract. Write the difference.

11 – 5 = [6]   13 – 8 = [5]

12 – 12 = [0]   16 – 7 = [9]

14 – 5 = [9]

15 – 3 = [12]

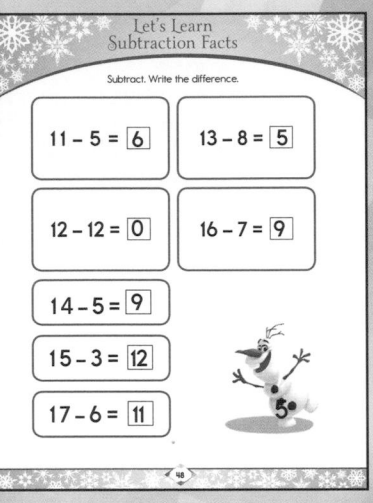

17 – 6 = [11]

48

Let's Match Facts

Subtract.
Write the addition fact that helps.
The first one is done for you.

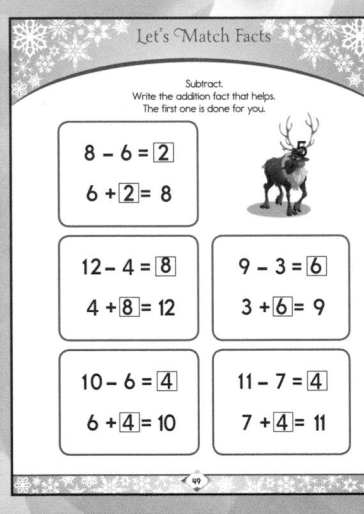

8 – 6 = [2]
6 + [2] = 8

12 – 4 = [8]
4 + [8] = 12

9 – 3 = [6]
3 + [6] = 9

10 – 6 = [4]
6 + [4] = 10

11 – 7 = [4]
7 + [4] = 11

49

Let's Match Facts

Subtract.
Write the addition fact that helps.
The first one is done for you.

11 – 6 = [5]
6 + [5] = 11

15 – 8 = [7]
8 + [7] = 15

14 – 6 = [8]
6 + [8] = 14

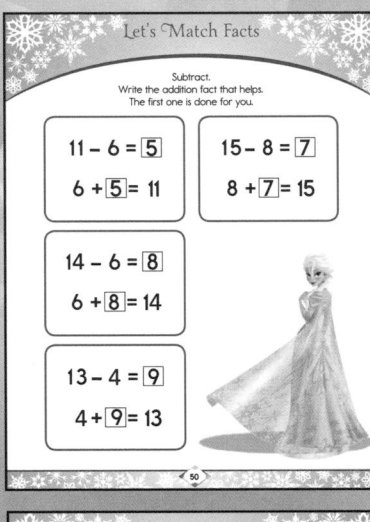

13 – 4 = [9]
4 + [9] = 13

50

Let's Match Larger Facts

Write the addition and subtraction facts.
The first one is done for you

3 + 6 = [9]
30 + 60 = [90]

7 – 2 = [5]
70 – 20 = [50]

8 + 2 = [10]
80 + 20 = [100]

9 – 5 = [4]
90 – 50 = [40]

10 + 70 = [80]

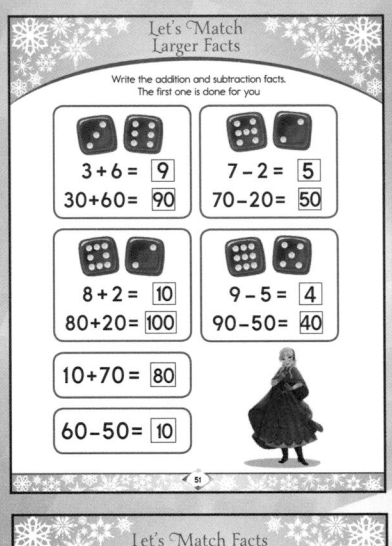

60 – 50 = [10]

51

Let's Race

Help Kristoff reach Anna before she freezes.
Record your time and the number of correct answers.
On your marks, get set, go!

11 – 7 = 4	13 – 9 = 4	9 – 8 = 1	10 – 6 = 4
14 – 1 = 13	100 – 50 = 50	8 – 7 = 1	11 – 4 = 7
9 – 6 = 3	9 – 4 = 5	7 – 6 = 1	12 – 3 = 9
9 – 7 = 2	15 – 2 = 13	10 – 4 = 6	12 – 2 = 10
8 – 6 = 2	20 + 60 = 80	11 – 2 = 9	9 – 5 = 4
14 – 3 = 11	11 – 6 = 5	16 – 2 = 14	10 – 2 = 8

Time to Complete: _____
Total Answers: _____
Total Correct: _____

52

Keep it up!

See if you can beat your score.
On your marks, get set, go!

30 + 30 = 60	15 – 3 = 12	10 – 8 = 2	12 – 5 = 7
13 – 3 = 10	15 – 1 = 14	13 – 2 = 11	16 – 0 = 16
13 – 1 = 12	11 – 3 = 8	12 – 1 = 11	11 – 5 = 6
12 – 4 = 8	14 – 2 = 12	8 – 8 = 0	14 – 4 = 10
16 – 1 = 15	40 + 30 = 70	90 – 70 = 20	8 – 5 = 3
10 – 3 = 7	9 – 4 = 5	80 – 40 = 40	19 – 4 = 15

Time to Complete: _____
Total Answers: _____
Total Correct: _____

53

Let's Match Facts

Subtract.
Write the addition fact that helps.
The first one is done for you.

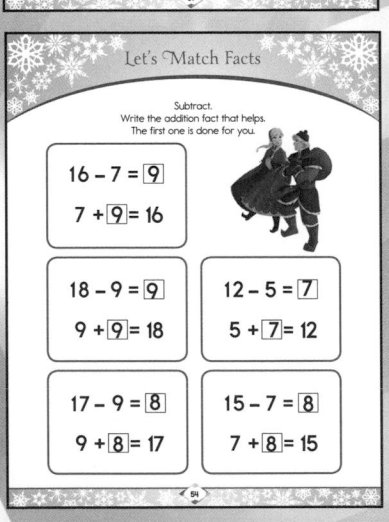

16 – 7 = [9]
7 + [9] = 16

18 – 9 = [9]
9 + [9] = 18

12 – 5 = [7]
5 + [7] = 12

17 – 9 = [8]
9 + [8] = 17

15 – 7 = [8]
7 + [8] = 15

54

72

Answers

Let's Solve Word Problems

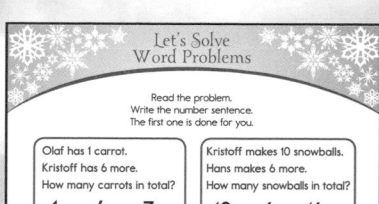

Read the problem.
Write the number sentence.
The first one is done for you.

Olaf has 1 carrot.
Kristoff has 6 more.
How many carrots in total?

$1 + 6 = 7$

Kristoff makes 10 snowballs.
Hans makes 6 more.
How many snowballs in total?

$10 + 6 = 16$

Anna has 10 dresses.
3 get wet in the snow.
How many are left?

$10 - 3 = 7$

Elsa makes 8 ice sculptures.
4 sculptures melt.
How many are left?

$8 - 4 = 4$

Sven has 14 apples.
He eats 6 apples.
How many are left?

$14 - 6 = 8$

55

Let's Add and Subtract

Add or subtract to find the answers.
The first ones are done for you.

add 3

IN	OUT
11	14
10	13
12	15
15	18

+3

take away 3

IN	OUT
14	11
12	9
11	8
18	15

−3

56

Let's Use a Graph

Look at the graph.
Answer the questions. Count the cells to help.

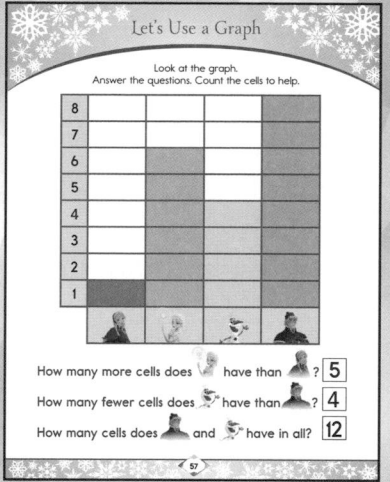

How many more cells does 🟦 have than ▮ ? **5**

How many fewer cells does 🟦 have than ▮ ? **4**

How many cells does ▮ and 🟦 have in all? **12**

57

Let's Race

Solve the problems.
Record your time and the number of correct answers.
On your marks, get set, go!

$14 + 2 = 16$	$15 - 2 = 13$	$12 - 5 = 7$	$9 + 9 = 18$
$10 + 5 = 15$	$13 - 1 = 12$	$14 + 3 = 17$	$17 - 3 = 14$
$8 + 8 = 16$	$12 - 3 = 9$	$13 - 0 = 13$	$12 + 1 = 13$
$10 + 4 = 14$	$16 - 2 = 14$	$11 + 2 = 13$	$8 + 5 = 13$
$9 - 7 = 2$	$10 + 6 = 16$	$13 - 5 = 8$	$14 - 4 = 10$
$17 - 0 = 17$	$12 + 3 = 15$	$12 - 4 = 8$	$7 + 8 = 15$

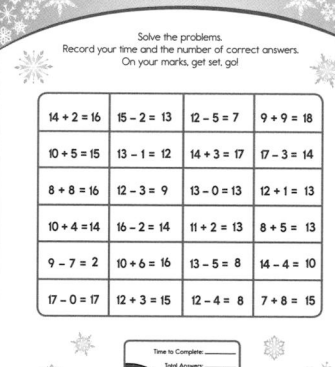

Time to Complete: _____
Total Answers: _____
Total Correct: _____

58

Keep it up!

See if you can beat your score.
On your marks, get set, go!

$9 + 5 = 14$	$12 - 3 = 9$	$14 - 3 = 11$	$7 + 1 = 8$
$10 + 3 = 13$	$16 - 2 = 14$	$15 + 1 = 16$	$12 - 6 = 6$
$9 + 6 = 15$	$11 - 3 = 8$	$15 - 15 = 0$	$8 + 7 = 15$
$6 + 8 = 14$	$15 - 5 = 10$	$14 + 0 = 14$	$9 + 9 = 18$
$17 - 7 = 10$	$5 + 6 = 11$	$11 - 7 = 4$	$11 - 4 = 7$
$13 - 6 = 7$	$14 + 4 = 18$	$16 - 7 = 9$	$10 + 2 = 12$

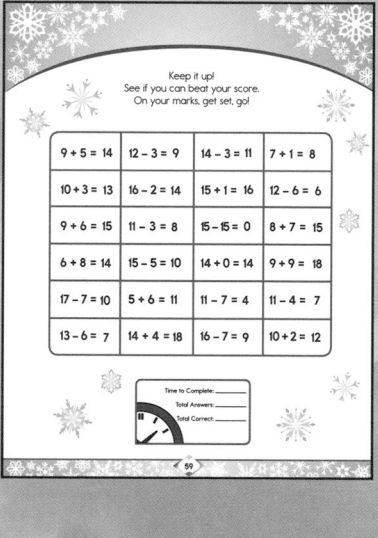

Time to Complete: _____
Total Answers: _____
Total Correct: _____

59

73

Here Are All the Things I Can Do

Put a snowflake sticker next to the things that you can do.

I can ...

Show different ways to make numbers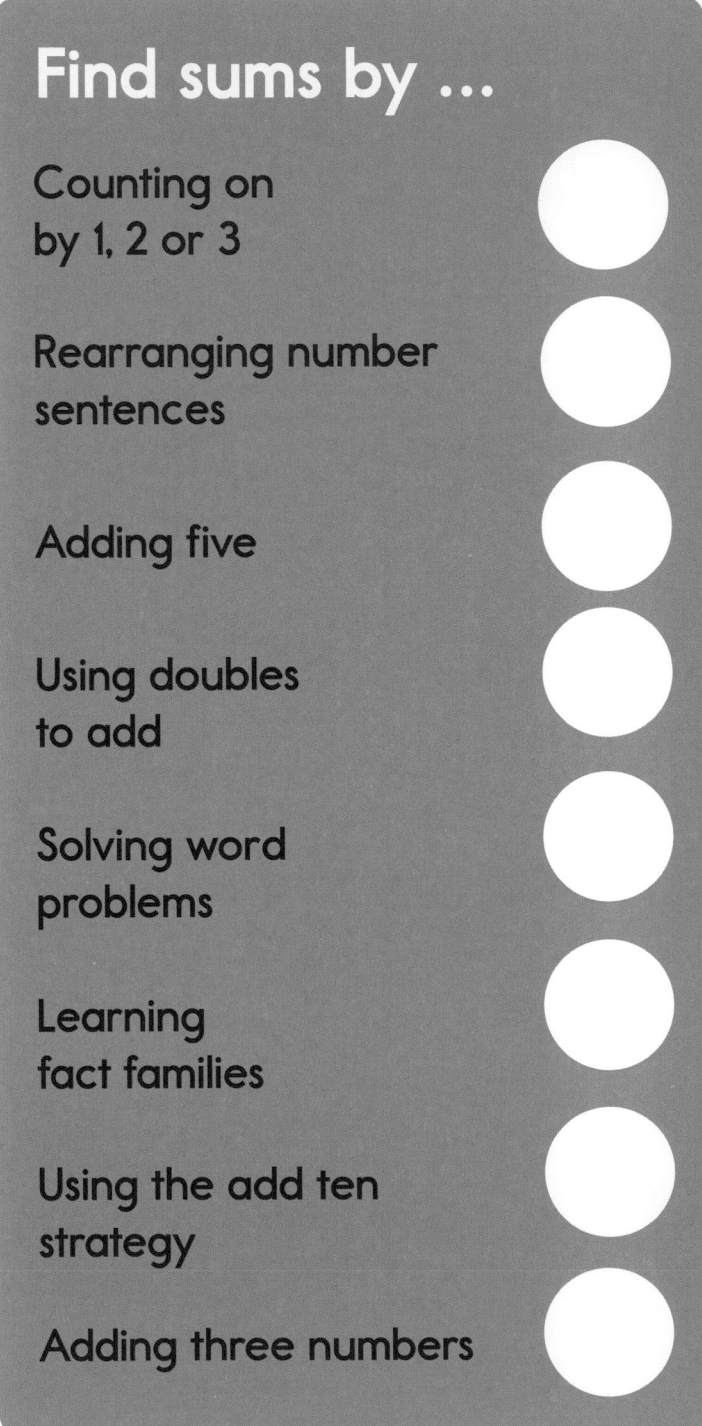

Count by twos to add and subtract

Count by fives to add and subtract

Count by tens to add and subtract

Use a number line

Use a graph to add and subtract

Find sums by ...

Counting on by 1, 2 or 3

Rearranging number sentences

Adding five

Using doubles to add

Solving word problems

Learning fact families

Using the add ten strategy

Adding three numbers

Find differences by ...

Taking away

Counting back
by 1, 2 or 3

Using doubles
to subtract

Solving word
problems

Learning fact
families

Finding larger
fact families

How does your child learn?

Research shows that all children benefit from a wide range of learning activities. Here are a few exercises to do together to strengthen your child's understanding of basic addition and subtraction concepts.

Tell maths-fact stories

Say a maths fact aloud, such as 2 + 1 = 3. Ask your child to use characters from *Frozen* to tell a story that illustrates the maths fact. For example, Anna was out picking flowers. She picked two flowers. Then she picked one more. Anna picked a total of three flowers in all.

Playing games makes learning maths facts fun!

Put together a basket or box with materials such as dice, dominoes, playing cards, pencils and other materials for maths games. Plan a special night every week to play some of these maths games.

- Play games with dice. Ask your child to roll two dice. As your child rolls the dice, call out 'add' or 'subtract'. Then ask your child to quickly add or subtract the two numbers. Switch roles.

- Play games with dominoes. Place sixteen dominoes face down. Each player picks up a domino and calls out the sum of the dots. The player with the higher sum takes the other player's domino. The player with the most dominoes at the end wins the game.

- Play games with playing cards. Remove all the face cards (aces, kings, queens and jacks) from the deck. Mix up and distribute the cards evenly. Each player draws two cards from his or her pile and adds the numbers together. The player who has the larger sum takes all the drawn cards. The player with the most cards at the end wins the game. Vary the game by finding differences – the player who has the lower number takes all the drawn cards.

Make and solve number puzzles

Work together with your child to make tic-tac-toe games where the sum of each row, column and diagonal is the same. Use each number only once.

Here's an example for the number 12.

7	2	3
0	4	8
5	6	1

Do a maths-facts challenge

Give your child an index card. Say a number, such as fifteen. Challenge your child to list at least five different maths facts for that number. Repeat with numbers up to twenty.

9 + 6 = 15   10 + 5 = 15   7 + 8 = 15   15 − 0 = 15   20 − 5 = 15

Hide-and-seek maths

Place ten small objects, such as buttons or beans, on a table or counter. Then hide three objects in your pocket. Ask your child to look at the number of objects on the counter to figure out the hidden amount. Ask, 'What do you need to make ten? Guess how many beans I have in my pocket?'

Subtraction hopscotch

Use coloured chalk to make a hopscotch grid on your footpath. Write ten subtraction facts on index cards. Mix up the cards. Draw one card and try to toss a stone in the square that shows the answer to the subtraction fact. If your stone lands in the correct square, hop to that space. If your stone does not land in the correct square, say a fact which has that number as the answer. See how long it takes to hop to each of the squares on the path.

Real-world doubles

Open up a carton of eggs and look for the double: six plus six. Point to a calendar. Ask your child to look at two weeks to find the double: seven plus seven. Hold up your hands: five plus five. Look at bicycle wheels: one plus one. Make a competition to find a certain number of doubles in your house.

Make up rhymes for maths facts

- Let's not be so late. Two plus six is eight.
- Please don't trip on sticks. Three plus three is six.
- Five plus five is ten. Let's do this again.